OUR
LADBABY
JOURNEY

OUR LADBABY JOURNEY

Success, Sacrifice & Sausage Rolls

MARK AND ROXANNE HOYLE

SPHERE

SPHERE

First published in Great Britain in 2024 by Sphere

1 3 5 7 9 10 8 6 4 2

A CIP catalogue record for this book
is available from the British Library.

ISBN 978-1-4087-3418-6

Typeset in Warnock by M Rules
Printed and bound in Great Britain by
Clays Ltd, Elcograf S.p.A.

Papers used by Sphere are from well-managed forests
and other responsible sources.

Sphere
An imprint of
Little, Brown Book Group
Carmelite House
50 Victoria Embankment
London EC4Y 0DZ

An Hachette UK Company
www.hachette.co.uk

www.littlebrown.co.uk

To Phoenix and Kobe, never give up on your dreams.
Love, Mum and Dad x x – R.H. and M.H.

Introduction

Before we get started, we want to thank YOU – yes, you! – for picking up our book. We're pinching ourselves that it's finally here and the thought of people reading our story is completely insane.

Hopefully you won't want to put it down again for a little while yet . . .

For those who know us well, we are forever grateful for all the amazing support you've shown us and our family on this crazy journey so far. We flippin' love the fact that people come to us to laugh and to feel joy. Together with you, we have created something truly special and we are thrilled to have you as part of the LadBaby community.

You guys are the reason we do what we do. And for those of you who are new here, where on earth have you been?! Just joking. Welcome, all of you. We're over the moon to have you with us, so buckle up!

This book is something we've wanted to write for a while. We're a normal family with an extraordinary story and it's one we're really proud of. But it's never felt like the right time to get it all down on paper before now.

When we were putting out our Christmas songs year after year, raising money for the Trussell Trust and public awareness of food banks, it was far too important to take time away from that project to tell you about us and our family.

It would have also been impossible to think of writing an autobiography when we didn't feel like we were at the *end* of that journey.

Making the difficult decision last year not to go for any more Christmas number ones (our Guinness World Record-breaking fifth in a row in 2022 felt like a good time to stop), it was as if we'd completed that chapter and were now at the beginning of a new phase.

A good opportunity, if you like, to have a look back over what has been the craziest of rides and a chance to reflect on how on earth we got here in the first place.

Because we still can't believe it ourselves!

Just a few years ago we were terrified new parents, winging it at life and struggling to make ends meet.

Today, we have thirteen million followers across all our channels, we've been part of five unbelievable charity Christmas number ones, published six best-selling children's books, been crowned Celebrity Mum and Dad of the Year and launched a hit podcast. We've even eaten sausage rolls with Sir Elton John. Yep, that actually happened!

So you could say that we've crammed a rather large amount into a very short space of time.

But while lots of people know LadBaby and LadBaby Mum, not quite so many of you know Mark and Rox. You'll have seen a few minutes of our life that we put online each week, but there's a lot more to us besides that.

And so we're going to tell you everything: from the days before LadBaby was even a thought in our minds, to the madness of these life-changing last few years. The good, the bad and the downright bonkers.

We know that people watch our channels for light relief, and we always make sure our platforms are fun places to hang out, but we want to be completely open in this book. We both think that's important.

And the truth is, it hasn't always been easy behind the scenes and there have been some incredibly tough times which have knocked us for six. As we started to experience a bit of success, we quickly learned that there's a darker side to everyone knowing who you are, and it's something we've had to learn to navigate. We're still learning.

We've had so many false and, frankly, hurtful stories come out about us in the press and online and we want to be honest about some of the harsh realities of internet fame.

You'll be hearing the whole truth right here, directly from us, for the first time.

There were hardships to overcome even before all this started. Both of us are dyslexic and school was a real battle for many reasons. Plenty of people thought we'd never amount to anything.

Because of all that we've been through to get here, we hope there's something for everyone in our story. If you're going through a rough time; if you've ever been told you can't do something or that you're not cool or smart enough; if you feel like you don't fit in and you're not meant to be here; if you want to change something but you're scared about making that leap, then we'd like to think our book is for you.

All the above has applied to us several times over, but we try to live by the mantra: don't get mad, get motivated.

At no point 'should' any of this have worked for us. But it did. We went out there, tried something (while also having a lot of fun!) and somehow we pulled it off. And if that message of believing in yourself and never giving up can help some-one else – if we can offer even a tiny bit of hope – then we'd consider that a win.

But you know what? Most of all, we want our book to give you a really good laugh. Finding the humour and making each other smile is how we've come through some of the most difficult times in our lives. We feel so lucky that we each married our best friend, and whether there's been heartache or happiness, we've always had laughter.

We can't wait to share all of that with you.

We've written the whole book together, so you'll be hearing from both of us throughout – first one and then the other. So, settle down, grab a sausage roll (what else?) and a cuppa. Shall we get started?

Yes, mate!

Prologue

Friday 21 December 2018

Mark

There was no way we were going to do it. Not a chance.

Ariana Grande was an MTV Music Award-winning, multi-million-record-selling international megastar whose fourth album had just gone double platinum. We were a couple of knackered parents from Hemel Hempstead with a novelty song about sausage rolls.

And yet, what had started off as a crazy idea to raise some money for a charity we cared about had spiralled, and we'd somehow found ourselves at the centre of a chart battle for the Christmas number one.

Rox

Mark had been vlogging as LadBaby for a good couple of years by this point and we'd built up a big and very loyal following. But even though releasing a Christmas single seemed to catch people's imaginations, any chat about topping the charts was ridiculous.

Mark

We'd also been told confidentially two days before that it was pretty much impossible. In terms of sales, 'We Built This

City' (our parody of the 1985 classic by Starship, where we'd changed the lyrics from 'we built this city on rock and roll' to 'we built this city on sausage rolls') was a good twenty thousand behind Ariana, who had been at number one with 'Thank U, Next' for the previous six weeks. We were never going to close that gap in forty-eight hours! It was mission impossible.

But it *did* look like we'd be safely coming into the top ten – possibly even top five. And we were buzzing with that.

Rox

Every step of the way we'd been told to 'manage' our expectations. There had been a lot of what I would call snobbery from people in the music business. No one said it outright, but there was a heavy implication that this industry was exclusive and people like us weren't welcome.

We'd even been written off in a big article by the BBC music reporter Mark Savage, which was headlined: 'Sorry, but LadBaby won't be Christmas number one.' How rude!

Mark

Weirdly, I think that article galvanised a lot of our fans and followers.

Rox

They were like: 'How dare you?! They're raising money for charity!' Seemingly accidentally on his part, Mark Savage ignited a fire in the British public and that piece ended up helping us because everyone wanted to support the underdog.

Mark

On the day of the Official UK Top 40, we travelled into central London to do a series of interviews ahead of the countdown that evening. We had to pre-record two different reactions – one for if we got the top spot and another for if we didn't. The plan was to get all of that in the bag and then rush back to Hemel where we were going to go live on our channels as the host Scott Mills counted down on Radio 1.

But disaster struck. There was a climate change protest outside the BBC studios and security locked down the whole building. With us in it.

Rox

We were held there for *hours*. We had the children with us as well – Phoenix was two and Kobe just six months old – so I was panicking that I was going to run out of nappies, milk and snacks if they kept us much longer.

Mark

The police were there, security was going mad and we were just waiting and waiting in BBC reception as the clock ticked on. We were supposed to be popping into the record label for a little celebration before heading home, but by the time we were finally released – three hours after locking down – we had no choice but to hotfoot it back to Hemel as quickly as possible so we could catch the countdown. We burst through the front door, turned on the radio and went live with our followers.

Rox

When you look at that footage now, you can see how grainy it is because it was literally Mark holding the camera in selfie mode while we bounced around our living room. It was not slick in the slightest and the audio is all over the place, but it was raw and absolutely real.

Mark

We could see the thousands of people joining us on the stream, the counter kept climbing up and it felt like we had the nation behind us.

Rox

The Front Room Massive!

Mark

By this time, I was just happy that we'd done an amazing thing. We'd raised money for the Trussell Trust and that was worth celebrating no matter where we placed. Earlier that day we'd even been thanked by one of the bosses at the Official Charts Company for 'bringing the excitement back to the Christmas countdown', which was incredible to hear.

When we were growing up, the Christmas number one had been a huge deal, a real moment in the calendar each year. East 17, Mr Blobby, the Spice Girls, Bob the Builder.

Rox

Icons, all of them. Especially Bob.

Mark

But it had lost a bit of its sparkle – *The X Factor* had it sewn up for so many years, which had made it all quite predictable. Clean Bandit had nabbed it in 2016 and Ed Sheeran in 2017, but neither of those were 'Christmas' songs.

Rox

Our daft track and the charity element behind it were a hark back to old traditions and I think people liked that.

Mark

But as far as we were concerned, we hadn't got number one.

Rox

We were like: 'Sod it. Let's just open a bottle of fizz anyway', as the numbers logging on to be with us via the stream continued ticking up. Forty thousand, forty-five, fifty. It would end up being the biggest live we've ever done.

Mark

We were getting messages from people saying they were in the kitchen with their family, rooting for us. Everyone just wanted us to do well, and that made me really emotional. I've got goosebumps now just thinking about it.

Rox

We were welling up before Scott Mills even got to the top ten. With each song – Jess Glynne, then Wham!, then Mark Ronson – there was no sign of little old us. He reached the top five and I was on pins.

Mark

It was Halsey at number five and Mariah Carey at four, and as 'All I Want For Christmas is You' faded out, I felt sick with nerves. Who was going to be number three?

Rox

Well, let me tell you. It was only Ariana bloody Grande! She'd fallen two places from last week's number one.

Mark

Which meant it was between us and Ava Max's 'Sweet but Psycho'. It was either one or two.

Rox

Scott Mills really built it up. It felt like it took for ever.

'So,' he said, 'this week, you have streamed, downloaded, viewed or bought either Ava Max or LadBaby to the Christmas number-one spot ... Let's do it'.

My heart was beating out of my chest.

Mark

Then the voiceover declared: 'This is the UK's official Christmas number two . . .', and we heard the opening line of 'Sweet but Psycho'.

Rox

It actually took me a couple of seconds to figure out that this meant we'd done it. We were the Christmas number one! And then I screamed very loudly because that is my default reaction when I can't comprehend what the hell is happening.

Mark

I burst into tears. I couldn't get any words out; I was rendered speechless. Rox flung herself at me and we held each other, both of us sobbing. At some point I managed to say thank you. Thank you so much to every single person who was with us and who had helped us pull off this unbelievable feat.

Rox

The two of us setting out to get the Christmas number one was as crazy as saying we were going to aim for an Olympic gold in the hundred metres. Like, that was never going to happen in a million years. But then it did! I can't put into words how surreal it felt.

Mark

When we came off the live, we stood there in silence in a complete state of shock.

Rox

We had about a minute of that before it all kicked off. The phones started pinging. And the doorbell went – all the neighbours piled round to celebrate. 'You've done it! You've done it!' People were turning up on our doorstep with champagne.

Mark

The local radio station came round with a big bunch of flowers, wanting a quick interview. It became a madhouse for the next few hours.

Rox

I was hyperactively joyous all night. I don't think it sank in until a few days later.

Mark

We did have a laugh thinking about poor Ariana Grande, who had been the hot favourite. We imagined one of her beleaguered management team breaking the news to her that she'd been knocked off the UK Christmas number-one spot by some family in Hertfordshire singing about sausage rolls.

Rox

She must have been so confused, bless her. We pictured her googling 'sausage roll'!

But wow. What had we just done? This sort of thing didn't happen to people like us. Mark was still working full-time as a graphic designer and doing LadBaby with me on the side.

Mark

I'd done the promo for the single while juggling my nine-to-five, carrying out interviews on the phone to MTV or Channel 4 News while standing on the fire escape of my office building. I'd had to beg my manager for a couple of hours off one afternoon to do a live chat on E4 Music. I'd raced there and then raced back to work again. Mental.

Rox

People used to see LadBaby as a joke. They'd say to Mark, 'How's your little video-making with the missus going?', and could be quite disparaging and undermining. Achieving something like this proved everyone wrong.

Mark

I'm not one of these people who believes in manifesting . . .

Rox

. . . neither of us are manifestators!

Mark

I just don't think that's how you make s**t happen. But I am a big advocate for self-belief and working hard to turn dreams into a reality.

Rox

At the time we were swept along, and I don't think we truly understood how momentous it was until a bit further down the line. There was no time to process it.

Mark

It was such an overwhelming time that it was hard to take it all in. We had built an incredible audience online of families and parents, but somehow this song and the charity it represented had reached the mainstream.

Rox

People outside of our online followers now knew about LadBaby, the Trussell Trust and 'the sausage roll family'.

Mark

We'd never contemplated that happening and what it meant, and I don't think we were ready for it. It had been a silly idea. Let's get a sausage roll song in the Christmas chart, make everyone laugh and raise a bit of money for a charity we really care about. It was that simple, that's all it was ever supposed to be.

It will always be one of the proudest moments of my life and the start of a new journey we never saw coming.

1

Young at Heart

Rox

I was always adventurous as a kid. Colourful, happy, playful and carefree, I'd say. I'd hang upside down from trees, go tearing through the streets on my bike and joke with the neighbours by playing knock down ginger with my younger sister.

I suppose you could say I had some boldness about me. I was independent and liked to stick up for myself.

Mark

Some things never change, right?

Rox

I guess not! But as childhoods go, mine was pretty good. Almost hippy-ish, really. My mum and dad were open, positive and super relaxed with how they raised me and my sister.

Mark

Rox's parents are both great. Her dad has always got a barbecue going and his guitar to hand with a song all ready to belt out. He's like Sting crossed with David Brent.

Rox

Ohhh Mark, he'll kill you for that! He's just an easy-going bloke and obsessively musical, my dad. He had a suitcase of little percussion instruments and the house was always full of music. It's probably why I have this weird ability where I know every word of every song ever written.

There was always a crazy mix of music going off because my parents would play everything from Queen to Abba to house music to Frank Zappa.

In fact, my earliest memory is watching Live Aid on the telly on that boiling hot day in the summer of 1985. I was only sixteen months old, but I can see myself standing on the sofa wearing a yellow romper as my mum and dad whooped along to Freddie Mercury in his all-white get-up. That's literally my first memory of life.

Mark

Rox is actually named after 'Roxanne' by the Police.

Rox

Well, there's a bit of debate about that. I think when my dad realised that the song was about a prostitute, he changed the story and told me that it was after some Hollywood actress instead. But I reckon it's the song.

Mark

It's *definitely* the song! Your dad's a huge Sting fan. Tell them your middle name, Rox.

Rox

My middle name is Zee.

Mark

After ...?

Rox

After ZZ Top, of course. Who else?

Mark

How brilliant is that?!

Rox

That's my mum and dad for you. Oh, and we also had a Labrador called Bootsy after the American guitarist, producer and singer Bootsy Collins. Bless his heart, Bootsy was such an amazing dog and we used to call him our brother.

Anyway, I was born Roxanne Zee Messenger and I came into the world, no doubt making a right old noise, on 2 March 1984 at London's King's College Hospital. Mum and Dad lived in a tiny flat in south London at the time, but about a year after I was born, we moved down to Kent so we could have more space and a garden.

I grew up in the lovely village of Farningham in a two-up, two-down on a crescent with a green. My sister came along soon after we moved there and the two of us shared a bedroom with bunk beds until Mum and Dad put a little extension on the house and we got our own rooms, around the time I was finishing primary school.

My little sis is two years younger than me – the same gap as our boys Phoenix and Kobe – and, believe it or not, she was always the cheekier one. She would be the naughtiest and get us into trouble.

Mark

Which is hilarious because it's a total role reversal now. Like, the complete opposite.

Rox

God yeah, these days she's well serious, super intelligent and running companies – she sees me up to all sorts on the internet and she's just like: 'Oh, Rox! What *have* you done now?!'

But when we were kids she'd do really mischievous things like shoving toast into the VHS video recorder (admittedly after being dared to do so by me), which would destroy it. I think my poor dad must have got through about twenty video recorders over the years thanks to the pair of us.

I remember I used to lower her down the stairs by her legs so she could watch telly from the stairwell when we were supposed to be in bed. Mum and Dad would be in the living room with *EastEnders* or *Corrie* on the box, blissfully none the wiser.

We also invented this great game where I'd put her in a cardboard box, sit her on a neighbour's doorstep, ring the bell and then I'd run off. Haha! I mean, we weren't terrorising the neighbourhood or anything, but everyone knew who the Messenger sisters were.

She was always academic, while I was much more creative, but we were very close. And still are. We both loved Take That and the Spice Girls, and plastered the walls of our bedrooms with posters. I also, randomly, had one of Michael Owen.

Mark

Michael Owen? I bet you didn't even know who he played for!

Rox

Course I didn't. I wouldn't have a clue.

But god, I loved Take That. I was mad about them. I was part of the Take That fan club, I had a little Filofax with prints of all their autographs and I'd record the songs on to blank C60s from the Radio 1 Top 40 countdown on a Sunday afternoon. You know when you'd press the record button at the start of the track? And then the trick would be to stop the tape recording before the DJ started speaking again. I had all my cassettes carefully labelled and I'd play them endlessly.

Mark
Who was your favourite member of Take That?

Rox
That changed on a daily basis, but it was usually Mark Owen.

Mark
Not Gary?

Rox
No! It was never Gary Barlow. Sorry, Gary.

Mark
How about Robbie?

Rox
Hmm. For quite a long time I was very angry at Robbie because he had the audacity to leave the band in 1995 and, to be quite frank, he ruined Take That. I've just about forgiven him nearly thirty years on. I never saw them live as a kid and so when we were invited in 2023 by Radio 2 to come and watch them perform at an 'intimate' gig, that was the stuff bucket lists are made of. I bawled my eyes out all the way through 'Never Forget'. What a moment.

Mark
I have such funny memories of that day. Everyone else was sitting watching the boys' performance very politely while Rox was on her feet, jumping around and belting out every song.

Rox

We were sitting next to Anton Du Beke (I know, our life is very random) and he was like: 'Go on, girl!' I think that song really hit me, though, with everything that's happened to us over the last few years and the lyrics about not forgetting where you've come from.

Mark

Which neither of us ever will.

Rox

Although I loved Take That, my biggest crush was probably the Spice Girls. Me and my sister would do the whole choreography for 'Spice Up Your Life' out in the garden on a Friday night for Mum and Dad, who'd be sat there dutifully clapping along. For the big finale, we'd stand on the back of some plastic chairs and then jump off into a flip and handstand.

Mark

Could you recreate that now?

Rox

Haha! Not without ending up in A&E.

Mark

Mel B actually followed us on Instagram at one point.

Rox

She did! I loved Mel B because she was so feisty. What a woman! And I had a bit of a Posh obsession because she was so quiet and mysterious. And Geri, of course, in that Union Jack dress at the Brit Awards in 1997. Legend.

Mark

It's always very surreal when someone you've loved and admired for years starts following us.

Rox

Like when Missy Elliott reshared one of our videos. All right, fair dos, she was laughing *at* me for my dancing, but I loved it.

Mark

Stormzy was pictured celebrating his number-one single and album in January 2020 with a cup of tea from one of my 'Yes Maaaate' merch mugs. That was bizarre. And we're still in touch with Ed Sheeran after the 2021 Christmas number one we had with him and Elton John.

Rox

Casual!

Mark

It's lovely, but we don't really get starstruck any more.

Rox

You do become a bit desensitised when you realise they're just normal people. Although when I met Ronan Keating to record the 2020 Christmas single, that was pretty hardcore because I had all the Boyzone posters and it was unbelievable to think that I was in a studio singing with someone I'd idolised as a kid. Someone I used to watch on *Live & Kicking* and *Top of the Pops* and read about in *Blush*, *Shout* and *Smash Hits* magazines. Remember them, girls? All the classics.

Mark

Actually, I did get a bit starstruck with Scott Mills when I met him. I spent my uni years driving between Nottingham where

I lived and Loughborough where I studied, and I'd listen to Chris Moyles in the mornings on the way there and Scott in the afternoons on the way back. I was so excited to go into Radio 1 for the first time in 2018, but he didn't seem that interested in this novelty act about sausage rolls because we're obviously not musicians. Although he wasn't rude, he appeared to me a bit dismissive, which I was a bit gutted about at the time. However, I've met him loads of times since then and he's been lovely.

Rox

We've got sidetracked, Mark. I fear this will happen a lot over the course of this book . . .

Mark

Sorry! Back to you, Roxanne.

Rox

Where were we? Oh, yes. So me and my sister spent a lot of time as kids just playing outdoors – it was that sort of child-hood where we'd go out on our bikes for entire days, with the only instruction from Mum being to come back for dinner.

No lie, we'd play pass the stick for hours. All this involved was getting a stick and riding around in circles in opposite directions passing it to each other. What a cheap day out! Every now and again, we'd mix it up a bit by putting the stick in the front wheel of the other one's bike which would mean we'd both fall off. Like, genuinely, that's what entertained us and we'd have permanent tans all summer from being outside all day.

Mark

Kids these days have no idea, do they? When Phoenix and Kobe's iPads die in the car, they don't know what to do with themselves even for ten minutes! When I say this, I'm totally aware that I'm turning into my parents (we all do eventually), but in *our day*, we had to make our own fun. On long car journeys, we'd watch the raindrops drizzle down the window and have a race for which one would make it to the bottom first. That was what passed for entertainment in the eighties and nineties!

Rox

I'm so grateful Mum and Dad gave us the freedom as kids to explore and have those adventures. They were always such amazing parents when I was little. My mum worked for a charity for years and never failed to find a way to fit it around the school run. She was so breezy about everything and, I think, very brave and forward-thinking as a woman at that time.

My dad, too. He worked for BT as an engineer and he put the hours in for us as a family. He grafted so hard.

Mark

I can't imagine your dad as a BT engineer! Although I can see him as a grafter. I've always seen him as a strong figure in your family.

Rox

But at the same time, he's so laid-back that he's horizontal! An old hippy at heart – he still goes to Ibiza every year on his holidays.

We were never well off, but neither were we ever poor. We just kind of muddled along in the middle and whatever worries my mum and dad had, they always protected me and my sister from them. I don't remember any negativity growing up.

Both sets of grandparents were around a lot and were key to making the whole family tick. They were the foundations. My dad's mum and dad, Joan and Bill, lived in a lovely house in Lewisham, south London, and they doted on me and my sister – we were their babies. We'd go there for weekends and I'd bloody love it. And oh my god, they were so cockney!

Mark

I was lucky enough to meet both of them before they died and, no word of a lie, going to their house was like walking on to the set of *EastEnders*.

Rox

''ello babe! You want some boiled bacon?!'

Mark

EastEnders meets *Oliver Twist* meets *Only Fools and Horses*. It was *mental*. I remember the first time I met them, the first thing Bill said was: 'Bloody 'ell 'e's tall, inny?' It was comedy. I didn't know people like that existed in real life. They spoke in actual cockney rhyming slang a lot of the time and it meant I only ever caught every third word of any conversation.

Rox

If you've ever seen the character Brick Top – the pig farmer – from the Guy Ritchie movie *Snatch*, well that was literally my grandad. He was a proper salt of the earth Londoner; he worked at a bakery and would bring the crusty bread home.

They were always smoking, him and my nan. I rarely saw them without a cigarette. And they'd come down to ours every Sunday and we'd go out for a curry – never a roast, mind. We weren't really a Sunday roast kind of family. It was always a Sunday curry, don't ask me why! There was probably some two-for-one meal deal on and that would be what swung it.

Nan and Grandad would take me and my sister to the caravan in Dymchurch on the Kent coast. We'd head off in my nan's orange Ford, the same one she kept for decades purely because it became tax exempt once it was twenty-five years old.

Mark

Rox's dad does that now – keeps all his cars because once they're more than twenty-five years old they're regarded as 'classic'. They're not 'classic', they're just old as s**t!

Rox

I loved those holidays at the caravan. Nan and grandad taught us how to play pontoon and chase the ace and, because I struggled with my maths (I was later diagnosed with dyslexia, which we'll talk about later in the book), they used to teach me how to add up with the playing cards. Grandad would bring a big jar of one- and two-pence coins and we'd play for money. My sister was constantly cheating!

My nan and grandad were the loveliest people and just everything to me. It breaks my heart they're no longer here.

Mark

I loved Rox's grandad to bits. But he was a scary individual. Very stern, although never with Rox and her sister.

Rox

He was just old school, but he was soft as anything with his grandkids. He couldn't function without the women in his life. But after he got Alzheimer's, it went downhill very quickly.

Mark

As the Alzheimer's took hold, he used to repeat his stories and what was so wonderful was that he'd get to the end of one that he really loved telling, roar with laughter and then that would reset him. And he'd tell it all over again. So we'd have these loops where he'd be telling me his favourite story about five times in a row, but he would get so much joy from it, that I'd be sitting there laughing along and enjoying these moments with him. We'd go round and round again.

Rox

After he fell and broke his hip in 2013, he deteriorated rapidly. He'd be there in the room with us, but he was gone. For someone who had been so full of life and such a character ... to then be so void and not present, it was devastating.

Very occasionally we'd get glimpses of the old Bill. In that December, I went to visit him in the old people's home and it was like I had my grandad back. I walked in and he was like: ''ello, babe! How are you? It's so lovely to see you!' After all these months of emptiness, he had this clarity and we were able to have an hour-long conversation, which felt amazing to me. I imagined it was like when someone dies and you just want them to come back even if it's just for an hour.

And then as I gave him a kiss and said goodbye, I saw him fade away again.

A couple of days later – and this is such a random thing – I was on the Northern line going home, feeling quite sad about my grandad because we knew he probably didn't have long left, and Santa Claus was sitting opposite me.

I say Santa Claus because this bloke honestly looked like the real deal. He caught my eye and said, 'It's gonna be all right, you know?'

At this point I was questioning whether I was hallucinating because, let's be real, having Santa offering you life advice on the Underground is not a normal thing to happen.

But it gave me a funny feeling, like a sign that something was about to change, and I got off the Tube, rang Mark and said, 'I think my grandad's going to go.'

And I was right – he'd passed away. That lovely conversation we'd had turned out to be the last time I ever saw him. My nan lasted a couple more years and then she went, too. I miss them both so much.

Mark

Before she died, Rox's nan got to meet Phoenix, who was born in 2016, and that meant the world to us.

Rox

And then my mum's mum and dad, Dot and Alf, lived on the Isle of Arran in Scotland. My nan was actually the mayor of Southwark at one point! No jokes. But they retired up to Scotland and me and my sister would be packed off to spend the summer holidays there with our nanny and grandad.

Mark

Wow, your clever old mum was on to something there, wasn't she? Sending you girls off for the entire summer.

Rox

We would absolutely live our best life up there. They lived in a cottage with a stream and next to what me and my sister thought was a full-on mountain, but was probably just a small hill. We'd go to the Glenashdale Falls and, again, we were always outside. As I said, those early years were all pretty perfect.

Mark

My childhood was quite different to Rox's. Very different, actually. We didn't have the hustle and bustle or the support of an extended family – there was only me, my mum, dad and my younger sister.

We had my dad's mum, but she was quite cold towards me – there was never a strong relationship, so she wasn't in my life much.

And similarly on my mum's side, it was all very fractured. She'd been brought up on the Aspley estate in Nottingham with two brothers and a foster sister, and although her parents were around, they weren't ever a huge part of my day to day. I just didn't really know my nana and grandad.

They were both heavy drinkers, and when my mum started her own family, I don't think she wanted them to be part of our lives.

Rox

When I first met Mark, I felt quite sad for him that he'd never had a large extended family growing up.

Mark

Well, you don't miss what you've never had. Having a big family wasn't ever something I craved because I didn't know any different.

There were no strong ties outside of Mum, Dad, me and my sister, and that, I suppose, made us a tight-knit team. It was us against the world. Not in a fighting sense, but in terms of love.

We knew we only had each other.

I was born on 12 April 1987 at the City Hospital in Nottingham and for the first few years of my life, we lived in a two-up, two-down middle terrace in West Bridgford, not dissimilar to Rox's family home.

My bedroom overlooked the fields and I still vividly remember the pale blue Mickey Mouse wallpaper and throwing bread out the window at night to the foxes below. Such a strange memory, but one that's stuck with me.

My sister was born in October 1990, when I was three-and-a-half, and I remember my mum going into labour because I was sent to stay at my nan's, which had never happened before and I don't think it ever did again, but at that moment, there was nowhere else for me to go. I can picture my nan and grandad smoking while I played on the living room floor with a toy Formula 1 car they'd told me my new sister had bought for me as a present.

That toy car made me think my sister was amazing before I'd even met her. She'd just been born and was already buying me gifts! I mean, what a great tactic.

Rox

Years later, we'd use that same tactic with the boys. When he was born, Kobe 'bought' Phoenix one of those toy car stacking ramps. He's long outgrown it, but we still have it because Mark is too sentimental to get rid of anything. Ever.

Mark

When my sister was about a year old, we did a house swap with a bloke across the street. We literally moved across the road because his house was slightly bigger and he was on his own and didn't need as much space.

Every single wall in the new place was painted black, there was no banister going up the stairs, the garden was overgrown and I remember Mum and Dad throwing themselves into tackling the house. They still live there today, so they've been there for over thirty years now.

Rox

My dad is still in our house in Farningham as well. I love that.

Mark

What can I tell you about Mum and Dad? They're working class, resilient, determined and very proud people. My mum has always kept a pristine house and, certainly on the face of it, has never let anything get the better of her. She's strong and gritty and she loves her family fiercely.

My dad is just as strong, although he's never been anything like as emotional as my mum. More than anything else, he's utterly dedicated to football and his beloved Nottingham Forest.

Rox

He's such a football fan, Mark's dad.

Mark

He really is. And with a relentless willingness to work. My dad worked every hour he possibly could, doing a job that he hated because he wanted to support us as a family. From leaving school he worked at a bakery factory in Nottingham, which is where he met my mum. Dad was in the bread department and she was based over in cakes and patisserie.

Rox

So, Mark is from a bakery background and I'm from a musical background and years later we would do a song about sausage rolls. I mean . . .

Mark

It was clearly meant to be! Our life is full of those funny twists of fate, as you'll see in this book.

The only time I ever really saw my dad worried was when he was made redundant after twenty-six years of working at the bread factory. It closed down in the late nineties and he lost his job – he'd only just got his gold watch for twenty-five years' service. I remember coming downstairs and seeing him looking troubled.

It was a huge shock, and I thought we were going to lose everything. For a while it was touch and go, and it looked like we might even have to move to another town for Dad to find work.

Rox

My dad got made redundant during the nineties, too. He ended up taking a job at a music college in London, which meant a cut in wages. Mum and Dad shielded us girls from the fallout at the time, but having chatted with both of them recently about that period, I understand now how difficult it was. My grandparents would help out with buying school coats and shoes and I do remember that but didn't grasp the significance of it when I was young.

Mark

Thankfully my dad got another job, at Hovis in Nottingham, so we didn't have to move and he stayed there for twenty-two years, I think. Half a century doing two jobs. I think that shows his work ethic and loyalty.

Mum stayed at home with us until my sister went to school. After that, she became – I can't write 'dinner lady' because she'll go mad – a school cook. We were a traditional working-class household.

Rox

I think Mark's parents got quite a shock when he brought me home for the first time. I was a fairly modern, loud, ambitious career woman and I'm pretty sure not the type of girl they thought he'd settle down with. I reckon I was a lot for his family to take in.

Mark

Er, you could say that! When I brought Rox back to Nottingham to meet my parents in 2011, she suggested the four of us go out for a meal together. My mum and dad said they'd meet us in Wetherspoons because they didn't really know many restaurants. We weren't ever a sociable, outgoing family like Rox's. We never had takeaways and 'eating out' was something you did for somebody's birthday and that would only ever be a trip to the carvery.

So this was a whole new world for Mum and Dad. They're both quite introverted and obviously Rox is very loud and annoying, haha!

Rox

You're welcome, darling! They probably imagined you with a nice Nottingham girl who was a bit more chill.

Mark

I'd say they were quite taken aback. But you grew on them, I think.

Rox

I just take a bit of getting used to!

Mark

Me and my sister were very aware that we didn't have the money for luxuries. If you wanted something, you saved up for it. Mum and Dad wanted to live in a decent area so they could get us into a good school and we'd have somewhere nice to grow up. But it meant they stretched themselves to the limit.

Mum would take on jobs she could do from home to make ends meet. She used to spend hours hand painting batches of toy metal soldiers to sell for what, looking back now, must have been only a tiny profit. She'd bake and sell cakes to friends and neighbours, anything to put a bit of extra cash in our pockets.

They'd put a little bit aside each week for our one holiday a year to the caravan in Skegness. Those times are some of my happiest memories, just the four of us.

Rox

I was so shocked when Mark said he didn't get on a plane until he was sixteen.

Mark

But again, I never felt that I was going without. It taught me that if there's a lot of love in a house – which there was – then that goes a long way. Cheesy, but true.

Because my dad was out working so much, it was Mum who did most of the bringing up of me and my sister. She was the constant. I think having my mum's influence is maybe why I'm much more in touch with my emotions than my dad ever was. Dad loved us, but he was never someone who would necessarily say it all the time. That's simply how it was – it's how he is as a person. He was like my best mate.

Rox

You tell Phoenix and Kobe you love them all the time, don't you?

Mark

Every day. They're getting to the stage now where they're a bit like: 'All right, Dad . . .', but I want to do things a bit differently with my own children. I want them to feel they can come to me about anything.

I'll ask them about their day and we'll talk about the three best things that happened and the three worst things, too. It was too much of a cringe to ask my dad about anything I had on my mind.

Rox

Because of the name 'LadBaby', there's this perception of Mark that I think might not be accurate. He's not a typical 'lad' at all. Mark has always been an equal partner in the parenting and running the house. He'll do the washing, the ironing, the bath-time and bedtime routines.

Mark

Where I did bond with my dad was over Nottingham Forest. That football club is the love of his life, and my entire existence as a kid became devoted to it, too. Football was everything when we had nothing, and every Saturday was centred around the Forest game.

Rox

Still is, babe. And don't I know it . . .

Mark

Because we couldn't afford to go to the matches, my dad used to steward at the City Ground so he could see the game without having to pay. Health and safety wasn't what it is now, and so he'd take me with him and I'd sit on the steps of the Trent End, watching the match. My mum gave me a little cushion to bring along which made those concrete steps a bit more comfy!

Match days were the best. Me and Dad would go for a kick-around in the park beforehand and then get to the ground two hours before kick-off so he could start his shift. I'd sit there happy as Larry because this was about me and him. This was our thing.

At the end of the game, we had to wait for the ground to empty before we left ourselves. Dad would go and hang up his yellow steward's jacket and then queue for a little brown envelope which contained his twenty quid pay.

Then on our way out, we'd stop off at the food stand and he'd buy a job lot of the leftover chicken balti Pukka Pies, which they were selling off cheap. I hated chicken balti – there were never any of the nice steak pies left! – but it didn't really matter. We'd walk home eating pies that had probably been sitting out for way longer than was healthy and I don't think I ever felt more content as a kid.

Rox

There's another one of our twists of fate in those pies, isn't there?

Mark

Fast forward to 2023 and I'd find myself creating a limited edition LadBaby Christmas dinner-flavoured Pukka Pie to raise money for the Trussell Trust. Just madness.

But for me, spending that time with my dad was so much more important than the pies or even the football itself. I actually get emotional thinking about it now. We'd experience the joy and excitement and the crushing disappointments of football together. Normally, the disappointments, being Forest fans. That was where the love was.

And I'll always thank my dad for that because it's still a part of my life today. Over recent years I've had the privilege of watching games in the Forest hospitality areas, and it's a very different experience to sitting on the concrete steps of the Trent End, I promise you!

Rox

Bless him, Mark tries his hardest to get the boys into football, but he's not had much luck so far.

Mark

Oh, my kids don't give a s**t! I even gave them Forest-related middle names – Phoenix Forest and Kobe Notts ...

Rox

Ahem, we'll talk about *that* later.

Mark

... but they're just not interested. They generally come with me once or twice a season and I have to bribe them with sweets to do that! Phoenix can usually get to half-time before he gets bored and asks for my phone. Kobe won't even be bribed with sweets most of the time.

Rox
I think you're very conscious not to force it, aren't you?

Mark
I'd love for us to be able to recreate the sort of memories I have, but I don't want to put any pressure on them.

Rox
What if they decided to support Derby County?

Mark
Then I'd never speak to them again! Joking of course. But we're lucky that both boys have loads of interests, love playing sports and they enjoy going to school.

That means a lot to me personally – another reason football became such a passion was because it provided escapism from the hell of school. School was a place I despised. It was a place where I struggled to keep up, never fitted in and where I was bullied for years.

2

Surviving School

Mark

School was an absolute s**tshow for me. I hated every single minute of it. I feel terrible for saying that because I'd never want to put my own experiences on to my kids and for them to be affected or influenced by what happened to me. They often ask what school was like for me as a boy and I can't bring myself to tell them the truth. I don't want to lie to them, but I keep all the details vague and say that it was mixed – sometimes I enjoyed it and others not so much.

But the truth is, it was year upon year of torture. An unrelenting onslaught of mental, verbal and sometimes physical bullying which wore me down until I didn't have a scrap of confidence or self-worth left.

Rox

I'd known Mark was bullied at school, but it's only recently that I've learned the extent of what happened. He finally opened up to me and it honestly broke my heart. I was horrified at what he went through.

Mark

I'd actually been quite happy at Greythorn Primary School, which was just a short walk from the family home. It was a nurturing school and the teachers were great, but even there, I'd never had what I'd consider to be a 'best friend'. I never even had a *group* of friends, to be honest.

At the end of Year Six, everybody had to choose a buddy to go up to secondary school with, someone to be put in the same form class as. Well, I didn't have one.

I remember being in the playground trying to convince this boy Fraser to be my buddy, but he already had someone else lined up. So I ended up being buddied with a kid who had just moved to the school a month before and who I didn't really know at all. That kind of set the tone and my friend-lessness continued into secondary school where it made me an easy target. I was a very solitary figure and an obvious kid to go for.

Rox

The thought of all this makes me so upset. Thinking of you with no one to buddy up with.

Mark

You could say that I was the epitome of an Inbetweener – I wasn't popular, I wasn't cool, I wasn't good enough at sport to be on the football team and I wasn't smart enough to be a nerd. I was a geek but without the intelligence. I was just … nothing.

And the dyslexia, which had been diagnosed in primary school, meant I really struggled with the work.

In a weird way, I always felt older in my head than my age. I used to find a lot of the behaviour of the other kids quite immature and silly and I had no interest in being involved in it. I was like a square peg in a round hole.

The school was in quite an affluent area of Nottingham and it was pretty obvious that the other kids had much more money than we did. They'd all have the latest trainers and the nice bags and pencil cases, whereas I didn't because we couldn't afford it.

Non-uniform days were the f***ing worst. It just became about who had the best clothes, which obviously I never did.

Rox

Urgh. Those days are always so tough for the kids from poorer backgrounds. So much pressure.

Mark

I used to turn up in normal uniform and claim I'd forgotten, because that was easier than spending the day in clothes that everyone was laughing at for being s**t.

I just couldn't make friends. I was terribly shy and wasn't able to go over to a group of people I didn't know and start talking to them. I didn't have the guts to do it and that made me vulnerable to the bullies. I was easy to single out because I was always, *always* on my own.

It was often things like name-calling and mockery and taking the mickey rather than getting physically beaten up, but it was *all* the time. All day, every day, grinding me further and further down and when you're suffering that sort of mental abuse over months and years, it diminishes you. I just shrank into myself.

There were constant comments like: 'Ah, Mark, do you have any friends today?' and they'd all burst out laughing. I'd spend breaks and lunchtimes walking around the school buildings, trying to look like I was going somewhere. I never was. I just had to keep moving and pretend I was busy so I could stay as inconspicuous as possible.

They used to play this 'game' in the PE changing rooms where they'd slap me on my bare back as hard as they could to see who could leave the reddest handprint. They thought this was hilarious and then I had to act as if it didn't hurt so that they didn't get any satisfaction or pay-off. I knew if I cowered or cried then they'd only laugh even more.

Rox

You were protecting yourself. It's survival mode, isn't it? I can't imagine how traumatising it must have been to go through that. I think of our boys now and can't bear the thought of it happening to them. The thought of it happening to *anyone* is just dreadful.

Mark

The changing rooms were rich territory for the bullies. I know I'm slim now, but back then I was a bit overweight and I'd get called fat. I remember taking my shirt off as if it was a race to the death because they were all waiting to see my bare belly so they could take the mick. I could never consider showering at school after PE. I couldn't. I'd just put my uniform straight back on.

Rox

Mark kept all of this to himself at the time. He never told a soul what was going on, not even his parents.

Mark

In my mind, with good reason. There had been an incident quite early on in Year Seven where I was deliberately tripped up in the corridor on my way to a German lesson. I'd landed on my face, which caused a nosebleed, and when I went to the office and they asked what had happened, I told the truth. This kid had stuck his foot out and tripped me on purpose.

My mum was phoned, his mum was phoned and I never really lived that down. From then on it was all: 'There's Mark, the little snitch. Are you gonna go and phone yer mummy?'

It was worse than ever, so I bottled everything up and kept quiet after that.

I also didn't want to make my mum and dad upset and worried ... it just made my life easier not to say anything.

I got used to being on my own, but I was very lonely. It was a very isolated existence. All I had was my mum, dad and my sister – there was never anyone else.

Home became a sanctuary. I loved being at home. The minute school was over, it was like a weight had lifted and I couldn't wait to get back to the safety of Mum, Dad and my sister.

But I definitely missed out on a lot of the key childhood experiences. I never had birthday parties as a kid because I didn't have anyone to invite. My mum would make me a fantastic cake and I'd get plenty of presents from them, but that was as far as it went. I didn't ever celebrate birthdays until I met Rox.

Rox

Birthdays were always HUGE occasions for me growing up. We'd have all the family and loads of friends and neighbours in the garden with a bouncy castle, a barbecue and a beige buffet.

Mark

That's totally rubbed off on me and now every year I have a party. I have no choice in the matter, to be honest! But it does feel like I'm making up for all those birthdays that I went without.

I sometimes wonder if I should have fought back, but I was too frightened. I would never have dreamed of hitting anyone. And the more my self-esteem was whittled away, the less capable I was of defending myself. What would be the point, anyway?

Rox

You did manage to get one over on them one time, though. I flippin' love this story.

Mark

There was one day when I saw an opportunity too good to miss. It was winter, there was snow on the ground and I spotted a group of the bullies on the school field with one of the main offenders standing there, holding court.

I scooped up a load of snow and a fair bit of ice and compacted it all into a perfect sphere. Now, as I've said, I wasn't any good at sport, but somehow out of nowhere, I managed to throw that snowball like an England fast bowler and it smacked my nemesis right into the back of the head. Bullseye.

No one saw me do it. I walked off as if nothing had happened and none of them ever knew it was me.

Rox

I'm so bloody proud of you for that!

Mark

Revenge felt sweet. They'd never have suspected someone as timid as me, anyway.

Rox

Hopefully he'll read this book and realise twenty-odd years on that it was you all along.

Mark

Funnily enough, plenty of them have been in touch since LadBaby took off, trying to be all chummy with me. Can you believe that? I'm always polite, but I refuse to enter into a conversation with them, even when I bump into them in real life.

Rox

It blows my mind the nerve of people.

Mark

I left that school the first chance I got and went to college. That was quite an unusual move because most kids stayed on for sixth form, but after my GCSEs they didn't see me for dust. And I've never spoken to a single one of them since the day I left.

I remember finishing my GCSEs and everyone was laughing saying they couldn't wait to see how badly I'd done. I told them they'd never find out because I wasn't coming back to sixth form, I was going to college. And a kid who had always been quite horrible to me asked what I was going to do.

When I told him graphic design at South Notts, he started laughing and said: 'South Notts College? The one on the council estate?!'

He told me he wanted to be a graphic designer as well and that he couldn't wait for ten years' time when I was going to be cleaning his office. Again, I didn't bother to fight back, I just let it go. But those comments and that scorn triggered something inside of me and spurred me on. It was a bit like: 'Fine, we'll see about that.'

And do you know what? Going to 'the college on the council estate' turned out to be the happiest times I've ever had in education.

Rox

You made some great friends, didn't you?

Mark

For the first time in my life, I had mates. I'd play football with them in the evenings and just hang out, things I'd never done before. I had people to talk to during the day and it just felt really, really nice. That's where I started to come out of myself. I found some self-belief and felt worthy of being liked.

Bizarrely, having been at a school where I was one of the poorest kids and being made to feel inferior because of that, now I was (comparatively) one of the richest. Because I lived in West Bridgford, everyone at South Notts thought I was posh! It was like the whole dynamic of my life just flipped and I went from being the poor kid to the rich kid. So odd. But those two years at South Notts were so brilliant for me and it was mainly down to the people. They were such a good influence in my life at a time when I really needed them. I've never thanked any of them for their friendship over the years, but without them, I don't know what sort of person I would be today.

Rox

They say those with the least always give the most, and that is so true.

Mark

I just wish I could go back and tell my younger self that it would all work out in the end. That it was always going to be OK.

Rox

You made it through, babe!

Mark

I did. I'm glad that I haven't had to speak to any of the kids I went to school with ever again. I'm glad they're not the people who have defined the rest of my life.

Rox

I think it shows Mark's character that he survived all that cruelty and emerged to make a success of the rest of his life. Mark never gives up on himself. He carried on moving forward and pushed himself on to better things, despite what people said to him or how they made him feel.

Mark

What it did was stir up a bit of grit in me and a determination to prove everyone wrong. All those kids who were s**t to me at school, I wanted to show them that I *would* amount to something and so I suppose it fuelled me. And continues to do so today. Surviving that bullying for so many years gave me a weird sense of inner strength because I never let them break me. That was how I coped with it. They never won because they never broke me. I knew that I could believe in myself even if no one else did.

Rox

Look at all the Christmas number ones. Everyone said, 'You can't do this!' And Mark was like: 'What are you chatting about? I'm gonna do it!'

The media and the music industry and plenty of people in our lives said it was impossible, but being told that he 'can't' is what sets Mark on fire.

Mark

Something interesting happened quite recently that really made me think about the past. One of the lads who was vile to me throughout secondary school – not the worst by any means, but pretty awful over a number of years – was really popular, brilliant at football and just an all-round Mr Cool.

Well, I saw him not so long ago working in a DIY store, cutting wood. Not that there's anything wrong with that, and

I don't know the full picture of his life! But I just found it quite amusing that this kid – this *bully* – who everyone thought was some sort of god and destined for greatness, didn't in fact go on to do all the amazing things people thought he would.

Rox

Karma's a bitch, right?

I never experienced the kind of horrendous bullying that Mark did, but I struggled at school from the start. I couldn't concentrate or focus and I never quite understood what the teachers were saying. If I was presented with blocks of text, I couldn't compute and would just zone out.

My mum had recognised something different about me quite early on. She's since told me I was in the kitchen aged about four – at this point I hadn't ever written anything – and I went up to the window and wrote my name in the mist, backwards and then forwards. Like a mirror image. As I started to learn to read and write, I'd always write backwards and on the wrong side of the page.

Mum was always very positive and determined that, whatever it was, we'd get to the bottom of it and find the right support. So, when I was in Year Two or Three at Anthony Roper Primary School, I had a test for dyslexia (a test that confirmed my mum's suspicions) and I'd also take extra vitamins and iron because she'd read that they could help. Both my parents had the attitude that this was going to be all right and wasn't going to hold me back, and they instilled that same confidence in me.

It was never hidden. They told me what dyslexia was and that it meant I might have to get some extra lessons and be given a bit more time to complete my work, which was totally cool with me. To me, these were all positive things, so I never thought of it as a negative. I was aware that I was different to the other kids, but brought up to believe that I was as normal as anyone else and this was nothing to be ashamed of.

Mark

I was in Year Three when I was diagnosed and it was down to a brilliant teacher called Mrs Drew, who I'm actually still in touch with through Facebook. She'd noticed some of the issues I was having with the work and had a conversation with my parents about getting me checked out for dyslexia.

I remember a bloke came out to the house and we had to go through this big form, checking every little detail, which would eventually lead to the diagnosis.

My mum cried when she found out. She was worried about what it meant for me and my future – she'd been so dedicated to me doing well at school so I could get a good job. She was desperate for me not to have to fret about money.

She joined the Dyslexia Association and would go along to these meetings, and she learned as much as she possibly could about how best to support me. As a result of my mum's commitment and Mrs Drew's guidance, I never fell behind at primary school.

Rox

My dyslexia presented itself creatively. I was always able to be visual and could stand up in a room and present until the cows came home, but I couldn't ever structure written sentences properly.

Isn't it funny that both of us dyslexics ended up becoming best-selling children's authors. I mean, it still blows my mind!

Mark

I'd been well supported at primary school, but secondary was a different ball game. My name was on this 'special needs' list, which meant getting pulled out of class for one-to-one help.

Obviously, this was like a red rag to a bull for the kids who were already making my life a misery. 'Oh, look at Mark, he has to go to the *special* class.'

I was teased mercilessly for being 'thick' and it was humiliating to the point where I invented this story that the school had made a mistake. I refused all the dyslexia support, including the extra time in exams, just to get them off my back.

Rox

I recognise some of that from my own experience and looking back at that time with the knowledge we have now around dyslexia, it was shameful really. My all-girls secondary school had this facility called a Learning Lab and, like Mark, you'd be called out of class in front of everyone, which would always feel a bit crap.

But I've got to take into account that it was more than twenty-five years ago. I'm sure the way kids are treated has moved on massively since then. I hope it has, anyway.

As I mentioned before, my sister was highly academic and she vowed that she was going to help me through. She came up with this ingenious idea where I would learn my times tables by bouncing on the trampoline in our back garden. So I'd be reciting them in time to the rhythm of the jumping and, honest to god, that's what drummed them in. With every school test I visualised myself on that trampoline and it jolted my memory into action. I must have looked like a right loon sitting there bobbing up and down in my seat.

Mark

I'm just imagining you doing that!

Rox

My dad taught me the planets to the tune of 'Bohemian Rhapsody' by Queen. 'Thunderbolt and lightning, Saturn's very frightening me, Oh Uranus!' and, literally, that's how I remembered.

We'd come up with these little strategies and I did what I could. My mum always said: 'Get the grades in the subjects you love. You don't have to get maths; you don't have to get French.'

Mark

'cause, let's face it, you can't even speak English at the best of times!

Rox

Exactly! But I loved art, cookery and IT. Even geography, because I was fascinated by volcanoes and tectonic plates. Anything visual, I could deal with and I enjoyed. Anything academic I was just awful at. But in the eyes of my family, that was neither here nor there. You got through it by doing your best. I was never judged and I didn't realise how lucky I was to have that unconditional and constant support.

I also had the gift of the gab, mind. And so if someone was going to make fun of me, I'd make sure I got in there first. I always had something better and wittier up my sleeve than any put-down they could come up with. I knew how to defend myself.

Mark

Those verbal skills and the ability to wing it have served you well in life.

Rox

Especially when I went into advertising and had to do PowerPoint presentations – I could always freestyle and talk my way round anything because that's what I knew how to do.

I wasn't a hugely popular kid at school, but I was fine with that. I had one good mate, Laura, and me and her would sit together in every class and try to avoid the crazy girls who were obsessed with boyfriends and boobs.

We weren't geeky or anything, but our attitude was, 'We'll just let you crack on with that while we sit at the back and get on with our work.' I wasn't interested in boys – I was never a tomboy, but I was always just mates with the lads rather than into dating them. I didn't have my first kiss until I was about sixteen. It was with a boy called Jason and we both had train-track braces that locked when we snogged, which was absolutely bloody hideous.

Mark

I think I was about seventeen when I had my first kiss. I was chronically shy and never confident around girls, so I was never going to be the college stud.

I also went through a ridiculously fast growth spurt around this time which came as a shock to everyone. My dad is 6 foot 2 and my mum is 5 foot 10 so we're a tall family, but within the space of a year, I'd outgrown both of them and was continuing to shoot up with no sign of stopping. My mum was worried and I ended up having tests at Queen's Medical Centre in Nottingham for Marfan syndrome, which is a disorder of the body's connective tissues and can be life-limiting. Not that anyone told me that!

It took a few weeks to get the results and I remember my mum being in tears, which was the first indication I had that this might be serious.

Thankfully the tests came back negative and my eventual height of 6 foot 8 was what I was always destined to be. It had just happened later and quicker than normal because of my bone growth, which was delayed and therefore younger than my actual age.

Rox

Mark's height is the first thing anyone ever talks about when they see him in real life. He's heard all the jokes about 'What's the weather like up there?' a million times before.

It's funny because you'd never go up to someone and tell them they're fat or comment on what a big nose they have. But people are quite happy to say, 'Bloody hell, you're so tall, it's freaky!'

Mark

It is odd. Height feels like the one aspect of physical appearance that people still think is OK to comment on.

But I've always liked being tall. To me, it's desirable. I wanted to be big, tall and strong and I always saw it as a positive. I suppose if I could choose, I wouldn't be quite as tall as *this* because it can make life difficult sometimes.

Rox

Beds can be a problem and buying shoes and jeans that fit is a pain.

Mark

Door frames as well. Standard frames are two inches lower than me so I have to duck every time. I've had to have cuts on my head glued three times because I've not quite made it.

But it's fine on the whole. And even though it makes me stand out in the crowd, I've never been self-conscious about it. My shyness never stemmed from my height.

Rox

Shy is not a word that you could have used to describe me. My love for the Spice Girls meant that I took on the Girl Power message. I believed it and I lived it.

And I had a power mum! I saw mum heading up the charity

she worked for and that inspired me. She always drilled it into me and my sister that if we wanted a career, we had to go out there and get it. She was like: 'You're not going to iron or clean for any man. You work hard and get yourself a career.'

And to this day, I still don't iron!

Mark
Or clean!

Rox

Be fair, Mark! I do the laundry! And I'm bloody brilliant at that.

But I had lots of strong, powerful women in my life who were all the bosses of their household and that has always stood me in good stead. From day one I was told to 'go for it, girl'.

I was always a bit overweight, but it never bothered me. I was the funny girl with a pretty face and I was comfortable in my body. That was Girl Power, right?

I felt I had enough personality to carry me. Maybe I was overcompensating. I'd wear lairy clothes (um, still do!) and I'd never shy away from putting on a swimming costume or a bikini. I had the best friends and we'd all raise each other up, which was bloody wonderful, thinking about it now. They're still my friends today.

Mark
It also shows that you've always stayed true to you. You've not changed.

Rox was the same as me, once GCSEs were over. She got out of school and focused on a subject she was passionate about.

Rox

I did well in my GCSEs and got grades ranging from A* to D, but I couldn't wait to dedicate all my time to art. As far as I

was concerned, I was going to be the next Tracey Emin. I'd
spent a lot of my lunch breaks in the art department at school,
using that time to sketch, which was one of my favourite
things to do. It meant that by the time I went to college for
an interview to do a National Diploma in art, I'd built up a
huge portfolio of work. My sketchbook was so big, it didn't
shut properly and so I stuck it in a Sainsbury's bag for life,
which my mum was horrified by. She thought it looked really
unprofessional! Everyone else had their lovely, neat books and
here's me with a bag from Saino's.

Anyway, I met this art tutor and got my work out on the
table. I used to do crazy stuff, it was all very 'out there' and
the teacher took a quick glance at my art and then looked at
me and said, 'You have a place here.'

And that was it. I was officially in my artist era.

Having so far charged my way through life, the world stopped
for me when Mum and Dad announced they were splitting
up. I think I was about sixteen and it was a proper shock. I
never saw it coming and it left me completely devastated. My
whole life was tipped upside down and everything changed
very quickly.

It's hard to know how to deal with it when when you're
only a teenager and you have precisely zero experience in
that area.

I'd had quite a nice life up until that point and I'd been
brought up with so much love, peace, happiness and joy. I was
shielded from a lot of what happened between my parents or
even what led to the divorce, but it felt like the rug had been
pulled from under my feet. It was hugely traumatic and I think
that's why a lot of my memories from that time are quite hazy.
I must have blocked it out. I do remember sitting on the floor
and crying, thinking: my family's gone.

I struggled to cope with the sadness because it was like

nothing I'd ever felt before. It was like: 'Whoa, what the f*** is this? It was a loss. It was grief.

Mum moved out of the family home and I didn't know what to do with myself. I wanted to help my dad, so I started by getting the house into some kind of order. I distinctly remember picking up a bin bag and putting the trash out, taking on jobs to help out.

Mark

I can't imagine what it was like to go through something like that at such a formative age.

Rox

I missed us all being together, holidaying together, playing music together. Suddenly life and everything I'd ever known ground to a halt and it was horrible. For a long time I hated them both, but it's true that time is a great healer.

Mark

Rox has always told me that throughout all the upset, her nan and grandad were her backstops. They were always there.

Rox

I loved hanging out at my nan and grandad's house. That became my hub and even though I was older now, I could be a kid again there and I'd sit in the garden eating bacon sandwiches with my nan.

It was a safe space for us when everything else felt so turbulent and uncertain. Even when I moved to London and got my first job, whenever life was too much or I had stress at work, I'd go straight to my nan's with my duvet and have a cuddle and everything would be all right in the world again.

My dad's now remarried and I have a step-mum and step-sisters, who are all amazing and part of my family.

Mark

I love all of Rox's family but especially my step-brother-in-law because he's a massive football fan and we have so much in common.

Rox

It was tough at first, though. When I'm going through something painful, my instinct is to keep myself busy. I've never curled up in a ball and wallowed. And it was during that initial period of turmoil that I decided what I wanted to do with the rest of my life. I didn't want to choose between my mum and my dad or live between two houses. I had to get away and so I thought: 'Sod it. I'm going to uni.' It was like a penny-drop moment. If I could get there, then I could start afresh.

No one in my family had ever been to university, but the two-year National Diploma I was midway through was a route to an undergraduate course.

At the time, the famous Tango advert was all over the telly – do you remember 'You've been Tango'd', with the orange man who went round slapping people? I pointed at the TV and said to my dad: 'I want to create things like that.'

Mark

Did you even know what sort of job that would be?

Rox

I was *clueless* about that. But I knew I wanted to be part of that world. It was the only plan I had besides the Tracey Emin one! Me and Dad started researching careers that involved making adverts and what qualifications you needed to break into that industry. He found that Buckinghamshire Chilterns University College offered creative advertising as a degree and, reading the prospectus, it looked perfect for what I wanted to do.

'There's an open day there tomorrow, Rox,' he said. 'Do you want me to take you?'

So we contacted the uni, said we were coming and the next day we got in the car and headed up the M25 for an interview. I took my big sketchpad with me and completely blagged it.

Mark

Had you upgraded to an M&S bag yet?

Rox

Ha! I actually hadn't – I think it was still the same Sainsbury's bag. But it didn't matter because I got offered a place to start that September and, a few months later, I moved into the student accommodation on the High Wycombe campus.

It was scary, but on the first day, this guy with glasses and curly hair came up to me and said, 'Shall we get a cup of tea?' and I said, 'Yeah, all right!'

He was called Nick and he went on to become a really famous and successful graphic designer. Over that cuppa, I knew I was going to be happy there. I'd found my people!

Mark

You were with creatives, see?

Rox

Exactly! Nobody here was going to make me do another fricking fraction again in my life.

3

Careering Ahead

Rox

Before I went to uni, I'd been worse than useless at every job I'd ever had. It wasn't that I was lazy, but I could never focus for long and ended up getting into all sorts of trouble. I had so many part-time jobs during college and I went through them like hot dinners.

Mark
Come on, babe, let's go through your glittering CV.

Rox

OK, deep breath! I was a florist at Bluewater, the big shopping mall in Kent. I had an eye for colours and so I was good at making up the bouquets, which I'd then have to deliver. But not everyone was happy to receive them, especially if they were an apology from a cheating boyfriend, and I had a fair few bouquets flung right back at me. And then I'd get too emotional seeing people upset. I couldn't hack it.

I also kept pricking myself on roses because I never learned to wear the gloves. I lasted a month.

Then I worked at a jeweller's that got robbed on my first full day in the shop. No word of a lie – three women came in and told me to stand where I was while they stripped the place bare. My mum had always said that human life was more precious than a wallet or phone and so I did as I was told and let them get on with it.

Mark
The owner asked you why you'd stood aside for them, didn't she?

Rox
Yes! She wasn't happy with me at all. But there were three of them and they were all massive. My mum and dad wouldn't let me go back to work there anyway. Not worth the risk.

I also worked in a newsagent's for a while, but I couldn't keep away from the Mars bars.

Mark
So, basically, you ate the stock.

Rox
I wasn't any good at focusing on *not* eating. Then I got a job as a golf caddy during the summer holidays from college. I had to deliver coffees and sandwiches to the golfers on the course and I'd tootle around in this little buggy. I loved that job because I got really good tips and I knew I could earn even more if I was able to get round the eighteen holes a bit quicker. So I modified the buggy to make it go faster, but unfortunately I made it a little *too* speedy and the thing chucked me out as I did a U-turn. I was thrown down a concrete hill, splitting my trousers in front of a group of gawping golfers.

Mark
This is priceless. Classic Rox!

Rox

Mortified. I hobbled back to the clubhouse, bleeding, in quite a lot of pain and thankful that I was going back to college the following week. I had no staying power in any job.

And with that track record, I know my parents were concerned about whether I was going to stick with a three-year university degree. But at Buckinghamshire I was doing something I truly loved and that's what made the difference.

I also instantly made a group of friends who became my family. After the first year, we moved out of halls and into a student house – I had my girl mates and we all lived in one place together and our boy mates lived next door with adjoining gardens and it felt like we were in a permanent episode of *Friends*!

I loved my course, but I also threw myself into partying. There was such a vibe in our student house – it was always fun and hilarious. A lot of the time it was complete carnage, mainly thanks to the student union, where you could get pints of snakebite for a pound.

Mark

I think snakebite's banned now?!

Rox

Er, if that's true, it's possibly entirely down to me and my mates.

For anyone who doesn't know, a snakebite is half a lager and half a cider mixed together in the same glass, and the concoction is *lethal*. We used to line up a Jäger train (basically, a long line of Jägerbomb shots), down them and then move on to the snakebite. Oh my goodness. And then I'd wake up in the morning, grab a coffee and go straight to lectures, right as rain. Ah, the energy, stamina and power of youth! Wish we could bottle it.

Mark

I can't say my uni days were quite as fun, unfortunately. After two years at South Notts College, I had the option to stay on for another twelve months to do fine art.

But university fees were due to treble the following year and that would have priced me out of going at all. If I was going to uni, I had to do it now.

I applied to Loughborough to study graphic design because it was close enough to Nottingham for me to commute there each day. It was about a thirty-minute drive, which meant I could stay at home and wouldn't need to take out a loan to pay rent.

Like Rox, I was the first person who had ever gone to uni in our family and Mum and Dad were tremendously proud. I can see now it was a huge achievement for someone like me with dyslexia and from a working-class background to get into such a respected uni and on to a highly competitive course.

But after coming out of my shell at college and having escaped the bullies, at Loughborough it reverted back to school and I was the odd one out again. All my course mates were privately educated – I was one of only a small few who had been to state school and there was a big disconnect there from day one.

I felt like a fish out of water and I knew they looked down on me. I wasn't being paranoid because within the first couple of weeks I'd been voted as having the 'worst accent' on the course, which was passed off as being 'banter'. On top of that, the tutor who had interviewed me for my place had since left and the bloke in his place simply didn't have the same rapport. I felt as if he didn't like me because he saw me as someone who didn't fit his course.

About three months in, he pulled me aside and said he could see I was struggling to keep up with the work.

'It's because you're not *cultured* enough,' he said.

I was a bit confused as to what he meant.

'What's your favourite film?' he asked.

'*Rocky*,' I replied.

He appeared to scoff.

'Why's that?'

'Well, I love the idea of someone achieving something against all the odds. And I also love Sylvester Stallone.'

The guy clearly didn't agree.

'Sylvester Stallone?! Stallone is your favourite actor? You should be watching *Breakfast at Tiffany's*. You should be educating yourself with *Rebel Without a Cause*. How can you expect to be a graphic designer and work in branding and advertising if you can't relate to people who are cultured?'

I stood there, not knowing how to respond.

'What's the last album you bought?' he asked.

'I think it was Eminem.'

'Your favourite Beatles song?'

'I'm not really a fan of the Beatles . . .'

'You don't even like the Beatles? Well, you're really going to struggle on this course.'

Rox

I just think that's unfair. That tutor had identified that Mark was finding parts of the course very challenging and he should have been offering him more support. Instead, he was questioning his musical taste.

Mark

I ended up failing three of the modules in the first year and, from there, I was given a choice. I could either resit the whole year or give up my summer holiday and redo all the work over the break. My tutor made it clear he thought I should take a third option, which was to walk away from the course entirely and do something else.

'I'll do the work over the summer,' I said.

And that's what I did. I worked really f***ing hard and I passed all three modules and made it to the second year. I continued to work my arse off and even though I scraped a 2:2 at the end of the three years, I had my degree in graphic design and no one could take that away from me.

On the last day, that same tutor called me into his office and asked me what my plan was.

'I'm going to get a job as a graphic designer.'

That's what I wanted to do. It's why I'd spent the last five years – two at college and three here – working towards that.

'And where are you going to get this job?'

'I live in Nottingham, so I'll start looking there.'

'Nottingham? Good luck with that,' he said. 'Let me know how *that* goes.'

Rox

Mark has come across these sorts of people throughout his life and it drives me mad. So much judgement. It shows his strength of character that he's never allowed them to drag him down.

Mark

I came from nothing, had a regional accent, a shaved head and I wore a football shirt. Maybe everyone assumed I was a thick football hooligan. I've actually grown my hair in the last few years and people definitely treat me differently than they did when I had a skinhead.

Rox

I find exactly the same with my weight. I've been bigger and I've been smaller and I'm treated totally differently between the two. We both know how it feels to be judged on appearance and dismissed, ignored or underestimated.

Mark

Like a while ago, when we went to buy a new car.

Rox

Prime example. I'd always wanted a cherry-red Jeep and so we'd saved a bit of money and we went to the showroom to have a look. I was beside myself with excitement because this was my absolute dream, but as soon as we walked in, I clocked the salesman looking us up and down. We asked if we could have a sit inside the car – Mark's 6 foot 8 and obviously needed to check he fitted in before we took it any further.

Mark

The guy made up some excuse about not having the key handy, so we asked if he could go and look for it. He then disappeared for the best part of half an hour while we stood there waiting. I think he was hoping we'd give up and walk out.

Rox

And when he eventually came back, he only opened the boot. He said we couldn't get into the car ourselves because he'd just had it cleaned and it was for some people who were coming in later who were actually thinking about buying it. He was so belittling. He was implying that us getting into the car for a couple of minutes was going to contaminate it. I can confirm that we'd both had showers that morning and were wearing clean clothes!

Mark

He'd clearly decided we weren't the sort of people who would be able to buy a Jeep and so he didn't need to give us the time of day.

Rox

I was upset at first and then angry. But people like him don't bother me any more. We've built a career on the fact that me and Mark are normal people, relatable to our audience, and we're proud of that. We'll never feel ashamed.

Mark

Absolutely not. And that university tutor just became another person to add to the list of people I've used to propel myself further on. Uni was a means to an end for me; it was about getting the education so I could start a career and, after graduation, I committed to applying for as many jobs as possible.

Rox

Like Mark, I was determined to do well at uni because my goal was always to get to London. And I knew how tough it was, especially for a woman, to break into a very male-dominated advertising industry.

I was constantly thinking about new ideas and ways I could get ahead. I had a weekend job in Sainsbury's working on the checkouts and I used to challenge myself to come up with super-quick advertising ideas for the beauty-related products I was ringing through the till. Shampoo, tweezers, whatever it was, my brain would be whirring and I had a little notepad where I'd write all these random thoughts down. I remember one time my manager came over and quizzed me about what I was up to.

'Roxanne, what on earth are you doing?'

I think it looked quite sus, like I was writing down customers' card numbers to clone them!

'Oh, I'm just jotting down an idea for an advert for Head & Shoulders.'

Which was true. But I'm sure she thought I was nuts.

I loved working there. Chatting to customers was my

favourite thing and it was the first job I managed not to screw up.

And then in the evenings me and my mate had a hair-clipping job for Claire's Accessories, which was fixing multiples of hair clips to the pieces of cardboard they're sold on. Mind-numbing stuff, but we'd get a cheap bottle of wine and sit in our living room, clipping until we'd made enough money to go out for the night.

To get drunk on snakebite, obviously.

Mark

Didn't you find a rat in the wardrobe of that student house?

Rox

Well, there were always plenty of mice because none of the landlords gave a s**t. The rent was a couple of hundred quid a month and it was dire.

Mark

So not a rat, then?

Rox

It was never officially verified as a rat.

Mark

You definitely told me it was a rat. Now it's been demoted to a mouse.

Rox

Rat, mouse, whatever it was! It was a rank house in the awfulest area, but it was all we could afford. I remember the smell of the place; it was like going into damp toilets.

Mark
Sounds lovely.

Rox
Best years of my life, mate.

Mark
This might sound mad given everything that's happened to us over the last few years, but working in Asda has been my biggest life-definer so far.

I'd taken some part-time shifts there during college and uni, and then carried on while I was applying for graphic design jobs and it's where I built a friendship group with the people who are still my closest mates today. Lasting friendships that have stood the test of time. We've all been there for each other through thick and thin and I'd never have met them had it not been for Asda.

I was there for seven years in total and I developed a rapport with the customers as well, which I think is one of the reasons me and Rox have managed to form such a good understanding of the public and why we connect with people.

After leaving uni, I asked for as many hours as Asda could give me and, over the next six months, wrote off hundreds of applications for graphic design jobs. I bought a book called *Advertising Now*, which contained photos of the most famous adverts from the last hundred years alongside the name of the advertising agency behind them.

I made it my mission to email every single one of those agencies with a covering letter and my CV. None of them ever replied. I was met with this wall of silence, which was demoralising. But I kept on plugging away.

Rox

While he was slogging his guts out doing this and getting nowhere, Mark almost ended up becoming a police officer. That's something I actually can't get over.

Mark

I'm the least likely copper ever. I run *away* from danger.

But this old boy had approached me while I was stacking shelves in Asda and said he was a retired superintendent. He told me that, with my height, I was built to be a copper.

'No one's gonna mess with you,' he said.

I told him I didn't have it in me. I might have the build, but I'm a total wimp at heart.

'Nah,' he said. 'You see, ninety per cent of policing is confidence. It's not about fighting, it's about presence, and if we stick you on a big horse, you're going to have that in spades.'

He told me he'd bring me in an application form and make sure I went to the top of the queue.

'You won't have to jump through all the hoops,' he said. 'I'll make sure your form goes to the right man and we'll get you fast-tracked.'

He was so positive and convincing. No one in graphic design was giving me the time of day. Maybe this was an opportunity I needed to take.

True to his word, the bloke returned with the form and I spent that evening filling it in. The day I'd arranged to hand it back to him, I was at work and my mobile rang.

'Is that Mark Hoyle?' barked a voice down the line.

'Er, yeah. Who's this?'

It was a guy called Simon Tomlin and he worked for Publicis, which was one of the big agencies in London I'd written to.

'I've got your CV in front of me,' he said. 'Even though you sent it to the wrong f***ing department.'

My head started spinning because he'd caught me completely off-guard.

'What do you want to be, Mark?'

'I want a job at an advertising agency as a graphic designer,' I stammered back.

'Then why didn't you send your CV to the HR department?'

'I don't know. I just sent it off to the address I found. I'm not really sure what I'm doing, sorry.'

'If you can be in London tomorrow morning at nine o'clock,' he said, 'I'll give you an interview.'

'Y-y-yeah. That would be great. Thank you. Um, where do you work?'

'Baker Street.'

'OK, I'll be there. See you tomorrow!'

Rox

Bloody Nora. Talk about a whirlwind. That's a lot to take in for a twenty-one-year-old lad! I bet you were all over the place.

Mark

I had to go and tell my boss at Asda that I couldn't come into work the next day and I caught the first train out of Nottingham at around five the following morning, desperate not to be late.

Simon turned out to be a really good guy – I'm still in touch with him now, actually. He told me that my blunder in sending my CV to the wrong department had worked in my favour. It meant that it had been passed directly to him, ending up at the top of a pile of papers on his desk, and he'd only decided to contact me first because my CV was the one right in front of him.

The interview went well and at the end of it he offered me a month's trial as a junior graphic designer.

'We can pay you a thousand a month. Can you start Monday?'

Bear in mind this was Friday.

'Yes, I can do that,' I said. 'Thank you.'

'Where do you live again?' he asked.

'Nottingham.'

'Notting Hill?'

'No, Nottingham.'

Simon raised an eyebrow.

'But don't worry,' I said, 'I'll make it work.'

'OK, see you Monday.'

I hurried away and immediately started looking at train times and fares for a daily commute between Nottingham and London. I didn't need a GCSE in maths to calculate that the grand a month salary wasn't even going to cover my travel costs.

I didn't know anyone in London I could stay with – I'd never even been to London before apart from a day trip to Tate Modern.

I asked Asda if I could work Saturdays and Sundays in order to top up my Publicis wages – between the two jobs, I worked seven days a week to keep my head afloat. I also took out a small loan, which helped.

Each morning Monday to Friday, I'd get the 6 a.m. train into St Pancras and then walk from there to Baker Street so I didn't have to pay for the Tube.

And I did that for six months because my trial was extended, but it almost killed me. In the end, I was almost relieved when Simon said they couldn't offer me a permanent position, even though it meant I had to start applying for jobs all over again.

Rox

Mark's work ethic is insane. I've never met anyone with the same ambition and drive to overcome any hurdles put in his way. He always finds a way to make things happen. When he started LadBaby, we didn't have Wi-Fi because we couldn't afford it and so he used to go down to McDonald's late at night and sit outside to cadge theirs while he edited and uploaded the videos. He did it every week for well over a year.

I love him with all my heart, but I also respect him more than anyone else in the world because, no matter what, he keeps going.

In all the time we've been together he has never ever let me down. He's never disappointed me. He's such a force and, during the hardest of times, he always tells me it's going to be OK. And because he says so, I know it will be.

Mark

It was another six months working back at Asda before I got a second bite of the graphic design cherry. By this time, it was late 2010 and I was offered a full-time junior role at a little agency based on New Oxford Street where they were going to pay £19,000 a year. This meant I could *just* about afford a tiny studio flat in London and I made the move from Nottingham to the Big Smoke.

My flat was in Hendon and it smelled of burgers thanks to being positioned above a pub called the Fernandez Bar and Grill, a classy joint that is sadly no longer with us. RIP.

Rox

That flat would end up being the first place we lived in together. Although we didn't know each other yet, Mark's new job meant we were now living in the same city and mixing in the same circles. It would only be a matter of months before our paths crossed for the first time.

I'd been in London since 2006 and was working as a junior art director at a company called Kitcatt Nohr. During my uni summer holidays I'd always volunteered for work experience at various advertising agencies, even if it was just coming in to make the teas. And it was through doing that and making lots of contacts that I was offered my first job.

All my uni friends had found work in London as well and we'd moved into a rented house in Muswell Hill.

Mark

Sounds posh!

Rox

Not exactly. It was the arse end of Muswell Hill, not the fancy bit.

We were all on junior salaries, climbing the career ladder and, after my rent, I had about £50 left a week to eat and drink. Me and my mates all looked after each other. If someone was short of cash one week, the others would chip in, that's just what we did. We were family.

I'd quickly realised that to get ahead in the media industry, you had to be there all the time and basically not have a life outside of work. I don't think uni prepared me in any way for the first year in the real world.

Sometimes if you were working on a pitch, you'd be in the office for twenty-four hours, grabbing a quick nap under your desk if you were lucky. I kept a beanbag and a duvet in the office. That was life in advertising.

Mark

It was the culture. You stayed late until the job got done. Nip home, get your head down for a few hours and then come straight back to work.

Rox

When we were pulling those all-nighters, the bosses would go get everyone a load of Domino's pizzas and we'd be happy.

Mark

It's incredible, isn't it? We could all be bought with a free pizza. Sometimes a crate of beer. That was all the incentive we needed to give up our entire lives to companies who should have been paying us a lot more.

Rox

Genuinely. A pack of Mr Kipling cakes and a bottle of wine. Haha!

Mark

I don't think you could get away with any of that these days. You hear about working standards now compared to what they were back then and it's completely changed, which is probably for the best. But when we were in the thick of it, you carried on until the death or you lost your job.

Rox

But those years are where I learned the most. Even if it was sitting in a meeting observing other people having a debate, I'd be taking little notes – on paper and mentally – and constantly finding out about how this world worked.

My first big pitch was for the World Wildlife Fund and a campaign to save the Amur leopard from extinction. The WWF wanted to raise awareness and sponsorship, and I honestly felt this endangered animal was going to die out if I didn't come up with a genius idea. The Amur leopard's very future depended on me!

I worked around the clock on this until the big day finally arrived. I had to walk into this room full of people from the charity and present my (hopefully) brilliant idea. The presentation was all very visual as that's how I work and at the end I revealed the slogan: 'Keep the World Wild'.

Mark

That's awesome, Rox. Love it.

Rox

Everyone in the room was silent and I waited for some sort of reaction. It felt like an age before they all applauded and the relief flooded through me. My boss told me later that the company had won the contract and it was down to the pitch and my rambling madness – 'Keep the World Wild' went on to be the line they used on all the branding.

I've still got the leaflet that had my slogan on it because my nan, bless her, kept it in a scrapbook. It was the best feeling. I'd done something really good at work and it was such a worthwhile campaign.

The imposter syndrome was real, though. I always felt incredibly lucky to be doing a job I loved, but it never occurred to me that I deserved to be there.

Mark

By the time I moved to London, Rox was already well on her way with her career. She was winning awards and gaining a reputation for being one of the industry's up-and-coming art directors to watch.

Rox

My boss at the time was very encouraging and had quite an influence on me – he saw something in me and took a chance. In 2009 he'd entered me for 'Young Spark' of the year at the DMA Awards, which were known as the BAFTAs of advertising, and the company flew me to Edinburgh for the ceremony. I just went for the craic. The company was paying and I was looking forward to having it large in Scotland for the weekend. It didn't even cross my mind that I would win.

When they called my name out as the winner, I was like: 'Holy s**t!'

Mark

I looked up the press cuttings from that awards do and – get this – the judges said: 'Roxanne stood out from the other candidates by demonstrating that she has a natural talent and real flair for direct marketing.

'It's refreshing to see so much enthusiasm and entrepreneurial vision from such a young marketer.'*

Rox

Even then I never felt like I deserved it. I just knew that I loved it and was going to keep putting out these wacky ideas and making my mum and dad well proud. Work made me happy, and I didn't mind the long hours and the competitive nature of the industry.

Mark

It was work hard, play hard.

Rox

Definitely. And it was on one of those 'play hard' nights out that a chance meeting with a (very) tall, handsome stranger meant things were about to get lively.

---

* https://www.campaignlive.co.uk/article/kitcatt-nohr-art-director-wins-dma-young-spark-award/967629

4

Fancy a Sambuca?

Mark

I'd never had any luck with women. My love life had always been a tragic mess and on the rare occasion I'd managed to land a date, it was usually a total disaster.

However, the night I met Rox was the most successful night of my life.

Rox

Right, this is so funny, because Mark is a classic Inbetweener.

Mark

Oh, here we go!

Rox

Come on, you've said it yourself. You are literally Simon from *The Inbetweeners*.

Mark

I tried really hard to impress girls. I'd wear a nice shirt, slap on the CK1 and make an effort on nights out, but it never really worked. I'd end up embarrassing myself and I always liked the girl who didn't like me back.

Being so tall made it hard work to chat anyone up, especially in a bar where there was loud music playing. From all the way up here, I often struggle to hear what anyone's saying and I have to stoop. Not a great look.

And the only shoes that fitted my size fifteens were a pair of shiny black lace-ups with a rounded toe bought from an old man's website. My funeral shoes.

Rox

You were so quirky, though! With your silky shirts and jeans. It was quite a style.

Mark

It wasn't a style, Rox. It was a necessity. And it clearly wasn't a vibe for anyone.

Rox

Ah, babe! Until that Thursday night, right?

Mark

Well, yes! Until then. There was a group of us from work going out for drinks as we often did and we'd been to a few nearby pubs before ending up in Jerusalem. That was a basement bar on Rathbone Place just off Charlotte Street and it was a total dive.

Rox

It was skanky, but it was cheap.

Mark

Cheap for London, anyway.

Rox

It was cheaper than anywhere else. There was always a happy hour where you could get two-for-one cocktails and that was the main reason I was a regular there. That Thursday, I'd had a bit of a day of it and my mate had said let's go and grab a happy hour drink to decompress. So, we piled down to Jerusalem and headed straight to the bar for our strawberry daiquiris.

Mark

By the time Rox arrived, I'd been in there a little while and had been talking to a girl – a housemate of one of the lads we were out with.

Rox

This is how everything could have turned out so differently.

Mark

We'd been getting on really well, chatting away and I started to think she was coming on to me. I mean, could she be? Surely not. This would be the first time that had ever happened in my life, which is why I couldn't work it out! No previous experience.

She told me she was a photographer around London and she shot for lots of magazines.

Rox

This is such bulls**t!

Mark

Ooh, jealousy doesn't become you, Roxanne! It wasn't bulls**t. She was a photographer and I thought she was the most incredible woman I'd ever met. We had a bit of a dance . . .

Rox

Oh my god, not your dancing!

Mark

Yep, I was pulling out all my signature moves. The legendary two-step.

Rox

I so wish I'd been there to witness that.

Mark

After a few drinks she said she had to go because she had to get up early to shoot a sunrise the following morning.

Rox

Haha! She was so bougie! The life you could have had, eh?

Mark

She gave me her number and said we should go out on a date at the weekend. Like, wow. I was on cloud nine. I went back to join the lads and I was on such a high that I said I'd buy shots for everyone. This was something worth celebrating!

Rox

Me and my mate happened to be at the bar when Mark came up to order the shots. We knew a few people from the group he was out with and so we were just having a natter.

Mark

I turned to Rox and said, 'Sambuca?' and she said, 'Sure.' Those were literally our first words to each other.

Rox

I hate sambuca but I liked the look of him. I honestly couldn't believe how tall he was!

Mark

And obviously incredibly handsome, right, Rox?

Rox

One of my friends was taking photos of the night, like everyone used to do back in the day, and they got a snap of me and Mark together. I'm not short – I'm 5 foot 6 – but next to him I looked titchy. I came up to his stomach.

And we've still got that picture. I look delirious because he was giving me all the feelings, but Mark looks ever so slightly scared for his life.

Mark

Admittedly, I didn't immediately fancy Rox or see her romantically because she'd arrived with a lad called Dan who I'd assumed was her fella.

Rox

He was actually a guy who I worked with.

Mark

So my first thought when she accepted the sambuca was, 'S**t, this is going to end up being a much more expensive round than I'd planned!'

Rox

He introduced himself to me and I said: 'Oh, Mark. I'm not a fan of that name. I'll call you M.'

Mark

Imagine meeting someone for the first time and telling them you don't like their name! She was so insistent, though.

'No,' she said, 'Mark doesn't suit you. You look more like a

Simon.' Which, weirdly enough, was the name my mum had originally wanted to call me.

Rox

God, I was a bolshy so-and-so back then, wasn't I?

Mark

Mark is a strong, reliable, Biblical name of great importance.

Rox

Hmm. Not feeling it. Ever since that night, I've called Mark 'M'. Sometimes 'Emmy'.

Mark

If we're working, she'll use Mark. But everywhere else it's M.

Rox

I remember we had a bit of a dance and he was all arms and legs. And I loved how awkward it was.

Mark

Awkward? Sorry, we were having a bit of a laugh and a joke and then Rox just vanished. I thought she must have called it a night and so I continued drinking with my mates until about an hour later, she reappeared out of nowhere looking a bit stressed out.

Rox

Oh god . . .

Mark

'I thought you'd gone home,' I said.
　'I can't do this!' she replied.
　'What can't you do?'
　'This! I can't do this!'

'Er, are you OK?'
I was so confused.

It was because I loved you. I just loved you instantly.

Mark
She said she needed some fresh air and started heading up
the stairs to go outside. I was totally oblivious. I followed to
check she was all right and then she turned to me and said, 'I
just really like you.'

Rox

I'd only had that one shot of sambuca and a cocktail, so I
wasn't drunk. I couldn't work out why I was so weirdly attracted to this guy.

Mark
Hang on. *Weirdly* attracted?!

Rox

Yes! Weirdly! You were all gangly and not my usual type.

Mark
You don't have to say *weirdly* attracted!

Rox

I was genuinely like: 'Oh s**t. What's happening here?' I'd
downed the shot, had a dance and then said to my friend that
we needed to move away.

  'I need some space,' I'd said. 'It's your mate, Mark. Like, he's
so . . .'

Mark
Weirdly attractive?

Rox

'He's so, I think he's . . . I'm just weirdly attracted to him.'

Mark

Stop saying weirdly!

Rox

At the time I didn't want to fall for anyone. I wasn't in the right place for a relationship. I'd been seeing a guy, it hadn't worked out and I was kind of done with it all. But I'd had such a strong physical reaction to Mark, like nothing I'd ever felt before and even though I tried to ignore it, in the end I thought, 'Sod it.'

And I went back.

Mark

I didn't know what the hell was going on. This gorgeous girl was telling me she really liked me and was now asking for my number. And this was the second time that had happened to me in the space of an hour. Was someone having a laugh? I was half expecting Jeremy Beadle to appear from behind the bar.

Anyway, we swapped numbers and Rox said that she thought I would ignore her texts and therefore I needed to add her on Facebook as well.

'I won't ignore your texts, believe me,' I said.

As if I was going to ignore her!

'You will,' she said. 'Now add me on Facebook.'

Rox

I just didn't really trust any man to keep his word. I was never 'the girl' guys wanted to chat up. I was always the friend of 'the girl'. Blokes talked to me in order to get to my friends, who were all really beautiful. I was the one who went out and partied, was always super career focused and was never in a serious relationship.

Mark

She said, 'Unless you add me as a Facebook friend, you're gonna ignore me.'

Rox

You're making me sound threatening. I wasn't violent about it!

Mark

You were pretty forceful, babe! There was a snag though, because I didn't have any data on my phone to log in to Facebook – this was way back when, before public places routinely had free Wi-Fi. I told Rox I had no data and she said: 'That sounds like an excuse. Buy some data now.'

Rox

Did I actually say that?!

Mark

You did! So I called up the network provider, asked if I could buy a gigabyte of data and then Rox took my phone, went on to *my* Facebook and requested herself as a friend. Then she opened up her own Facebook, held up her phone to my face and said, 'There, I've accepted you.'

Rox

Wow. I was either more hammered than I thought or a complete and utter psycho.

Mark

You were like no one else I'd ever met before. But I kind of liked it.

Rox

I remember at the end of the night, you made sure I got in a cab safely and you texted me, just like you said you would, on my way home.

Mark

I went home that night, a bit p***ed, thinking what do I do now? I'd finished the evening with two girls' numbers and this was unprecedented territory. They were both beautiful and I'd hit it off with each of them. Which one did I go for? But because I'd forcibly become Facebook friends with Rox, it was hard not to pursue her first.

Rox

That has got to be the most psycho thing I've ever done.

Mark

I'm obviously very glad you were such a psycho that night.

I was always far too painfully shy to talk to girls and so I think the fact that Rox had come into that bar with a guy I'd thought was her boyfriend meant I'd been totally relaxed. When we were doing those sambuca shots and dancing on the dancefloor, it never occurred to me that she could be interested and so I probably talked to her differently to how I might have done if I'd thought she was single. I wasn't trying too hard. I'd been myself.

Rox

I knew what love was and I'd been in love before. But when I met Mark, it was completely different from the get-go. I'd heard people talk about 'love at first sight' and all that jazz and I'd always thought it was a bit gimmicky and silly. But something along those lines genuinely happened for me that night. I was like, 'Whoa, I'm gonna marry you.' I just knew I was going to end up with Mark.

Mark

Because you were weirdly attracted to me.

Rox

You were just funny.

Mark

Good-looking, tall, handsome . . .

Rox

It was like meeting a best friend. It felt like we were meant to know each other. I'm not going to say it was definitely instantly 'in love', but it was as close as you can get. It was a very strong and genuine connection and I knew we were supposed to be together. And from that night to this day, we've basically never stopped talking.

Mark

Straight away it felt like we were family.

Rox

Yeah, that's what it was like. I didn't know why, but I *needed* you to be in my life. It was like: '*Yes!* You're the light and the energy I need here', and that's the best way I can put it. I know that sounds so weird, but it was a feeling of, 'Ah, *here* you are.' This all makes sense.

Mark

This works.

Rox

Let's go!

Mark

From that night, we were texting and Facebook messaging non-stop. I was hugely flattered because I'd never had any woman show me this much interest. I remember telling my friends that I'd met a girl and she *really* liked me and it shocked everyone. No one even tried to disguise their surprise.

Rox

Mark told me he was going to the football that weekend and that put me off a bit! I'm not from a football family, I didn't understand the game at that time and had never had any interest in it. So I was like, 'Oh no, he's a football boy . . .'

When he told me he was a 'Forest fan' I thought he meant he enjoyed walking in woodland. I had no clue.

Mark

Luckily, she didn't hold it against me. I think it was about a week after sambuca night that we went on our first date. We went to a pub in Islington and it felt like I'd known her for ever.

Rox

I was a bit nervous because I'd never enjoyed going on dates. I'm not a date person. It was a hilarious running joke with my friends about how much I hated the stilted awkwardness of it all. I just could not deal.

But there was none of that discomfort or cringe factor with Mark. We just chatted for hours and hours and hours, laughing our heads off the whole time. Mark's a very funny person to be around and I enjoyed his sarcastic humour. I also liked the fact he wasn't very 'male'.

Mark

Now, wait a minute!

Rox

Hear me out. I worked in quite a male-dominated environment and so I knew all about bravado and mansplaining. Mark was never like that. It was like two mates having a laugh, never once trying to outdo or impress each other, and I loved that. We had so much in common even though we were very different people.

Mark

I always tried to be funny to cover up nervousness and a lack of confidence. Even now I try to make light of everything because I feel more comfortable if something is amusing. But I never felt the need to do that with Rox, it was all very natural.

Rox

Whenever I'm nervous, I just talk.

Mark

Which meant trying to get a word in edgeways was a bit of a challenge on the date!

Rox

I just knew I'd fallen for him. And what sealed it for me was the hug I got at the end of the night. Getting an embrace from a 6 foot 8 man is wonderful because you're just engulfed in this lovely cuddle. I think it was the hug which made me tell Mark I loved him on that first date.

Mark

This is absolutely true. I walked Rox on to the Tube platform and as the train came into the station, I gave her this hug. The doors opened, she stepped on to the train and I thanked her for a nice night. And then she said, 'OK bye, I love you!'

Rox

Oh f***. I hadn't meant to say that, I'd just got all flustered and so then I tried to correct myself and only made it worse.

'Sorry, I mean … I don't *love* you; I mean … I really *like* you …'

Mark

I made a joke of it and said, 'It's fine, I love you too!'

'OK, thanks!' she replied. And then the doors shut.

Rox

Christ alive, I've tried to mentally block that out. What a cringe!

But I wear my heart on my sleeve, so that's exactly the sort of pickle I get myself into. And I did love him. My parents brought me up to be very emotionally open and taught me to tell people you love them because you might never see them again. That's just what I'm like.

Mark

Things moved quickly after that first date.

Rox

Like, scarily quickly. Although it didn't *feel* scary. It felt right.

Mark

Rox's rent had gone up and she'd had to move out of her shared house and was currently crashing on her sister's sofa while she found somewhere else to live. She'd been telling me that she'd have to look for a flat share which would probably mean moving in with a stranger, something she wasn't keen on. So, after only about a month of seeing each other, I asked if she wanted to come and move in with me. I know that seems hasty, but it made sense in so many ways.

Rox

The plan was to move into Mark's studio flat in Hendon and then pool our money to look for somewhere a bit bigger together. Just a few weeks after we'd met in Jerusalem, I turned up at his place with my worldly possessions packed into a couple of bin bags and a suitcase.

Mark

There was no storage in this studio, so Rox put all her clothes under the bed, which became her makeshift wardrobe. You might have seen a walk-in wardrobe, but have you ever seen a bed wardrobe?

Rox

Having my clothes stored under the bed meant every morning I had to lift the mattress to get to my 'wardrobe' so I could get dressed for work.

Mark

I honestly think we invented wardrobe beds. More people should have them.

I remember on that first night together, we went and got two KFC boneless banquets and watched telly together in bed.

Rox

KFC was our saviour on many occasions. The flat only had a microwave and a one-ring hob. No oven. You couldn't cook a meal and so whenever we had any cash left over on a Friday, we'd have a celebratory banquet.

Mark

To give you a picture of where we were living and what we were living in, the flat consisted of an IKEA sofa bed, that one-ring hob, an undercounter fridge, a sink, washing machine, a microwave and an ex-display TV I'd bought cheap from Asda. There wasn't even a nice view out the window, just a brick wall.

Rox
And it was always bloody freezing.

Mark
By the time Rox moved in, the pub downstairs had gone under and shut down and they turned off the heating for the whole building. For two months there was no hot water either, so Rox had effectively set up home in a flat above a derelict pub with no hot water and no heat. When she wanted to shower, I used to boil the kettle, mix it with some cold water and pour it over the top for her. I know how to treat a woman!

Rox
You say that, but I'd been in a house that had a rat, remember? So this was still a step up for me!

Mark
So it *was* a rat?

Rox
Not this again!

Mark
Sometimes I accidentally 'forgot' to boil the kettle and just poured freezing cold water over her and she'd scream the place down.

Rox
Always the joker.

Mark

There was one time the fire alarm kept going off. Because it was a former pub, there were these massive, very loud alarms and the only way we could stop them ringing was to physically lodge a dinner knife into the box. Every few hours the knife would fall out and one of us would have to get up through the night and wedge it back in again.

Rox

Good times, eh?

Mark

But one thing I loved about this terrible flat was the fact I could lie down in bed and open the fridge without getting up. I could grab the eggs and the bacon, put them on the hob while still lying in bed.

Rox

I'm not sure why, but the months we spent in that flat are some of my happiest memories.

Hendon was a lot further out than I was used to and we had to leave well early to get to work on time. It would take an hour on the bus, but I look back on those journeys now with so much fondness. During a time in our careers where both of us often worked late, that time together on the bus in the mornings was really special.

Mark

We just fell into this partnership very quickly. As soon as we moved in together, we got a joint bank account and combined our money. Both salaries went into this account and we shared everything.

Rox

I know friends thought we were moving too fast, but it felt right. We partied together, we struggled together. We were a team no matter what.

And even now, all our earnings go into one account and everything is split down the middle. There is no 'my' money or 'his' money.

Mark

We were carefree about everything. We were both in our twenties, living in London and having the most fun.

Rox

We didn't have any worries. Not compared to the responsibilities which come with having kids and a mortgage.

Mark

I love seeing Facebook memories when they pop up and the old photos that transport you back to a certain time. Seeing pictures of me and Rox from eleven or twelve years ago in that poky little studio flat is always beautiful.

Rox

I often look back to that time when we were so young and full of hope. It's a reminder that everything is going to be all right.

Mark

One of the things me and Rox had in common from the start was our love of a good prank.

Rox

We never filmed them back then, but the stuff we do for LadBaby is exactly what we've always done.

Mark

Growing up, I used to prank my sister a lot. She was terrified of spiders and so I bought a plastic one and it was the best thing I owned for about ten years. That spider was a gift. So I was delighted to discover that Rox was equally easy to wind up. She can be a bit dramatic.

Rox

I'll hold my hands up to that.

Mark

It doesn't take much to make her jump and when she does, she jumps out of her skin, screaming blue murder. Sometimes I'll innocently walk into the kitchen, not even intending to frighten her, and she'll leap ten feet in the air.

Just the other day, she was on the treadmill in the garage and she had her headphones on, singing her little head off. I honestly tried not to scare her because I didn't want her to fall off the treadmill and hurt herself.

'Rox?' I said, being really cautious. 'Rox? I'm in the room and I'm coming over. It's only me, so don't be alarmed. Rox?'

And then I just stood next to the treadmill and gently waved to get her attention. I started laughing because I knew it was going to happen. Sure enough, full-on scream as if she'd just come face to face with a serial killer.

Rox

I can't help it, it's how I've always been.

Mark

Discovering that trait was incredible. The endless possibilities!

Rox

This is what I have to deal with.

Mark

Because we'd often finish work at different times, one of us would get back first. If it was me, I'd text and ask Rox how close to home she was and then plan accordingly. When I knew she'd be arriving in a few minutes, I'd position myself behind the door or under the bed and jump out as soon as she walked in the room. It never failed.

Rox

He got me every single time. You used to get me with that fake bloody spider as well, planting it in cupboards and striking terror through my heart.

Mark

That never got old.

Rox

You did take it too far once, though. There was a line and you crossed it.

Mark

The one after the gym? That's still my favourite scare of all time because it caused such a reaction, but I honestly thought you were going to leave me afterwards.

Rox

I very nearly did, Mark. And I'd have been fully justified.

Mark

Fair enough, I accept that.

We'd both been to the gym and because I got changed first, I popped to the shop opposite to get some food. Rox still wasn't out and so I started walking back on my own. She rang me asking where I was and I fibbed that I was just at the flat and about to go in.

She said she was two minutes away and I saw the opportunity. I dived behind a car and waited, knowing she'd be coming past any second. I thought I'd give the game away because I was giggling so much and she'd hear me.

Anyway, along comes skippy, happy little Rox and I leapt out at her, all 6 foot 8 of me, arms in the air and roaring like a lion.

Rox

Oh my god. I have never been so petrified.

Mark

She screamed so loudly that the whole street echoed. And then she burst into tears.

Rox

I froze to the spot and was physically shaking.

Mark

I felt dreadful. I knew I'd f***ed it. I started apologising: 'I'm so sorry, I'm so, so sorry. It was supposed to be a joke.'

Rox

I'd honestly thought I was going to die.

Mark

She said, 'Don't you EVER do that again.' And I never did. Not outside, anyway.

Rox

In fairness, I did see the funny side eventually.

People ask how on earth do I put up with him, but from day one, our relationship has been about jokey banter, and he makes me laugh like no one else. This is how we've always done things; we completely get each other. Sometimes we literally can't stop laughing and it's the best thing.

We have this game where we give each other the middle finger in public, but we have to try and hide it. Although sometimes Mark just does it outright for the shock value.

Mark

Rox might be at the checkout at the supermarket and I'll just shout over, 'Rox!', she'll turn round and I'll flip the bird.

Rox

I always tell him we can't carry on like that any more, people know us now!

Mark

It's very childish and very basic. But doing that stuff at the most inappropriate times is what makes it funny.

Rox

We do it on planes, don't we? If one of us bags the single seat while the other one draws the short straw and has to sit with the kids, it'll be, 'In your face!' and a V-sign.

It's so silly, but it gives me *life*.

Mark

One bone of contention that could have scuppered the relationship in the early days was the fact that Rox smoked. I've never smoked – I've never done any drug harder than paracetamol – and it was the only thing I really couldn't stand about her. I loved everything else, but I absolutely hated that.

It used to really upset me and for the first few dates I wasn't sure if I could carry on seeing someone who smoked.

Rox

Both my grandparents smoked and I'd smoked since university. I also saw it almost as an essential part of my job – all the bosses smoked and there were many alliances formed and opportunities discussed over a ciggy break.

But I knew Mark detested it.

Mark

It came to a head one night when we were heading home from town and I remember Rox saying she couldn't wait to get off the Tube so she could have a cigarette.

'Why?' I asked. 'Why would you want to do something that's killing you? I want to spend the rest of my life with you and I don't want you to get lung cancer and die.'

Rox

I was shocked by how upset he was. Smoking was something we'd bickered about off and on, but I'd never seen quite how strongly Mark felt about it. It was like something switched in that moment.

Mark

She went into her bag and pulled out her box of Marlboro Lights, which had one cigarette left. She ripped the cig in half and threw the pack on to the seat in front of us and she said, 'Fine, I'll never smoke again.'

I just thought she was having a little tantrum; I didn't realise she was actually serious.

Rox

I've never smoked since. I'm quite a headstrong person and when I say I'm going to do something, I stick to it.

Mark

As we got off the train, I picked up the ripped cigarette and put it in my pocket. I've still got it today.

Rox

I told you before, Mark never chucks anything away. Such a hoarder.

Mark

It's sentimental. It's a reminder of what I think was a really pivotal moment in our relationship.

Rox

I think it's the only thing Mark has ever asked of me. And what swung it for me was his genuine show of care. I don't think I'd ever felt that from a partner before and although obviously I knew smoking wasn't a great thing to do for your health, I'd never had anyone spell it out so starkly that this could kill me. I'd honestly not thought of it in those terms.

So I did it. I gave up.

Mark

I couldn't believe she'd done that for me. It was another sign of the strength of our relationship. By then I knew that Rox was The One.

Rox

I know my friends and family were all quite shocked that I'd found someone I loved so much. Up until then I'd been so focused on my career and I'd always said I wasn't interested in marriage and didn't want children.

I'd been scarred by what had happened with my parents and the divorce – I didn't ever want to be in that situation myself and so I'd put the barriers up.

Mark

I think I helped Rox restore her faith in men. I was loyal, honest and devastatingly handsome – what more could she possibly want?

Rox

You joke, but you did, in a way.

Mark

She'd had that thing about not needing a man. And I don't think she did, but as a team we both worked better. I think I softened her harder edges and she realised she didn't have to do any of this on her own.

Rox

It all stemmed from the way I dealt with the breakdown of my parents' relationship. Or how I *hadn't* dealt with it, might be a more accurate way of putting it. I didn't know how to manage those feelings and so I buried them.

I'm much better at openness and expressing my emotions these days, especially with Mark. There's nothing we can't talk to each other about. But although we share everything, life is so busy that there's often not the time to reflect on whatever has just happened, which is why writing this book has been such a brilliant opportunity for both of us to dig into the past: celebrating the highs and coming to terms with the lows.

Having the space to look back and think about all these life experiences in a meaningful way – and doing it together – feels so positive.

When I met Mark, everything changed. Suddenly, I loved someone so much that I couldn't imagine life without him. And I also started reassessing my feelings about having kids, because I wanted to have Mark's children. I wanted to keep *not* wanting them, believe me! But I was helpless to those feelings, really. And I could see how much Mark wanted kids and I knew what a great dad he would be.

Mark

As a teenager, I used to babysit kids on the street for pocket money and I was good at it! I loved looking after kids and I'd always wanted children of my own, perhaps because I didn't have a big family growing up.

Rox

I was a selfish person before I met Mark. Not necessarily in a bad way, but I was very one-track minded in terms of my career. I'd had to be selfish in order to look after myself and get ahead. But I think sometimes people misinterpreted that directness as me being brash and loud.

Mark

You? Brash and loud? Never!

Rox

We were quite different characters, though, weren't we?

Whereas I was flippant, all about living in the moment and 'we-could-all-die-tomorrow-so-let's-just-do-crazy-stuff', Mark was much more responsible. He saved money rather than spending it on frivolities and he helped me think about financial security and the future a lot more.

Mark

I think we were both good influences on each other. Rox was always outgoing and a people person, but I found it hard to form close relationships because of my upbringing and experiences at school. Outside of my family, it was difficult for me to let anyone in emotionally, but Rox started opening me up. I started to discover some confidence for the first time in my life.

Rox

You were just quite shy and you'd use sarcasm as a defence mechanism. I think I encouraged you to relax, chill and enjoy life a bit more, and to be open-minded and not so constantly worried about money.

Mark

Money was always my biggest worry, as it had been for my mum and dad. I'd seen them agonise over it my whole life and so it was impossible not to carry that.

Rox

Mark always saw the worst-case scenario in any situation.

Mark

And Rox thought of the best-case scenario. I'd stress over the what ifs. What if we lose our jobs and then what if we have nowhere to live and then what if, what if, what if? And Rox would say, 'And what if we don't and we just party for ever?'
     We levelled each other out.

Rox

We found an equilibrium. Yin and yang.

Mark

We brought the best out of each other.

Rox

I knew I was going to marry you. It was just a matter of when.

5

The Things We'll Never Agree On

Rox

Mark is my soulmate. My BFF. My ride or die. There is no one I'd rather do life with.

Mark

Yep, same to all of that.

Rox

But that doesn't mean our marriage is all hearts, flowers and butterflies. What marriage is? We love each other dearly and deeply, but we're also very different people, as you're probably getting a sense of!

Mark

We're totally aligned on all the big important 'life' stuff – parenting, family, finances. But there are some things we will never ever agree on.

Rox

Because he's wrong and I'm right.

Mark

Do you want to put that to the test?

Rox

Is that a challenge?

Mark

How about we take some of the hot topics we are poles apart on and slug it out over these very pages?

Rox

Challenge accepted.

DISNEY: YAY OR NAY?

Rox

It's the most magical place in the world.

Mark

And the most expensive.

Rox

It's where memories of a lifetime are made.

Mark

If you're prepared to pay for them.

Rox

You can't put a price on memories of a lifetime, Mark.

Mark

Er, Disney can. And, it turns out, the price is thousands and thousands of pounds.

You can go and make equally nice memories feeding the

ducks in the park. Have a picnic, take a walk in the woods, make a day of it.

Rox

Or you can have castles and fireworks and Mickey ears. And even Mickey-shaped food.

Mark

In a restaurant that will charge you an obscene amount of money.

Rox

OK, I know you find Disney triggering because it hits you in the wallet and you think it's a rip-off. Tell you what – you go and feed the ducks and run around the woods and I will run towards the Disney castle.

Mark

Too expensive, too many people. Queuing up for three hours is not my idea of a holiday.

Rox

Now come on, you *willingly* queued up with your son (who didn't care in the slightest, by the way) to meet Buzz Lightyear and Woody, and you were happier than I've ever seen you in my life.

Mark

If you'd asked me if I wanted to spend the cost of a Disney holiday on three hours of queuing for Buzz, I would have saved the money and not gone. I love *Toy Story*, but not that much.

The films are fantastic, but they take the p*** when you go there.

You want that toy? That'll be a hundred quid.

Want to realise your lifelong dream of meeting Cinderella? Three-hour queue.

Rox

But, for me, the magic of Disney will always transcend the prices. I have wonderful memories of running down the road to the castle. It smells of vanilla sugar plums.

Mark

The castle is *so* disappointing. When you see it on the big screen, surrounded by sparkles and stars, it's a thing of beauty. And then you get there and you're like, 'Oh, really?' It's tiny.

Nottingham Castle is better. It's bigger, it's got heritage and a real hero in Robin Hood.

Rox

Are you saying Mickey Mouse ain't a hero?

Mark

No! He doesn't do anything! What's he ever done? Other than made a lot of money?

Rox

Mickey Mouse is a symbol of hope.

Mark

I've heard it all now.

Rox

Walt Disney was told he was no good, but he never gave up. He created Mickey in the face of adversity.

Mark

I'll give you that. Walt Disney did a great job; he fought to get his dream made into a reality.

Rox

He made a land full of magic for children.

Mark

I've got full respect for Walt.

Rox

You'd better have. Don't you dare slag off Walt.

FESTIVALS: HIT OR MISS?

Rox

Music, joy, dancing and freedom, that's what festivals mean to me.

Mark

Mud, misery and the overpowering stench of bodily fluids.

Rox

You haven't lived, Mark.

Mark

I had a pint of p*** thrown at me at V Festival. You call that living?

Rox

You're 6 foot 8, you were probably in the way and ruining their view.

Mark

There I was, looking forward to watching Plan B when I felt it hit my head and splatter all the way down my back. And when it's warm, you know it's not cider.

Rox

I've more or less given up with you and festivals now.

Mark

I don't fit in a tent and I get a bad back from standing.

Rox

You make a good signpost for when I get lost, though! And camping is part of the fun.

Mark

They invented hotels so we didn't have to sleep on the ground in sleeping bags on blow-up beds which deflate overnight.

Rox

Some of my favourite-ever live performances have happened at festivals. I saw Amy Winehouse in a tent at Benicàssim in Spain and it was one of the most incredible experiences of my life. I feel so privileged to have been there.

Mark

Go to a gig at an indoor arena, where the Portaloos aren't going to flood and you can go home afterwards and sleep in your own bed.

Rox

But you can't beat the vibes at a festival. And the choice of moving from stage to stage seeing loads of brilliant artists across one beautiful weekend of fun and frolics.

Mark

Better still, watch it on the telly in your living room where you have access to running water, a toilet, central heating, a bed, all your favourite food and drinks, and the best view, from every camera angle.

Why would anyone trade that in for getting pushed, shoved and elbowed in the face, and sleeping on the ground in a field full of people they don't know?

Rox

OK, why don't you just do that with the football? Don't bother going to the stadium, just watch the matches on TV.

Mark

If a festival lasted ninety minutes like a game of football, I could put up with it. I'm not going to bed down for the night in a football ground.

Rox

Mark, I would never expect you to camp at a festival because I wouldn't be able to take you moaning the whole time.

Mark

I'd be happy to take a VIP opportunity where they'd chopper me in and place me right in front of the stage and then take me back out again. But I'm not trekking across muddy fields to pitch a tent. 'Oh, I need the toilet. Let's walk for an hour to stand in a queue and pee in a bucket.'

Rox

The stories me and my friends have about festival loos over the years still make us cry laughing.

Mark

Revolting. Re.Volt.Ing.

GHOSTS: DO THEY EXIST?

Mark

Where's the proof?

Rox

They do exist.

Mark

I don't believe in anything you can't prove.

Rox

OK, what about when we got the Christmas number one and 'My Way' by Frank Sinatra, which was my grandad's song, came on the radio? That was a sign.

Mark

It was a coincidence.

Rox

Mark, that song only ever plays when there's a huge fricking moment in my life and it freaks me out because it's not exactly a recent hit.

Mark

Babe, it's the most popular funeral song in the world. It gets played all the time.

Rox

But not on Kiss FM!

Mark

It wasn't on Kiss FM. Be serious.

Rox

I genuinely believe in signs. And it's ghosts who send us those signs.

Mark

There's no such thing as ghosts. Do you believe in elves, leprechauns and unicorns? Dragons? Do you believe in dragons?

Rox

Yeah, I've seen *Game of Thrones*!

Mark

Tell me this. Why is it that all 'ghosts' are Victorian? Or headless on a horse? Where are all the ghosts on skateboards with baseball caps? Why do people never see ghostly figures knocking about in Manchester United tops?

Rox

You'll definitely be in a Nottingham Forest shirt when you're a ghost.

Mark

No I won't be, because I will be dead. When you're dead, you're dead.

Rox

If that's true, what's the point, then? What's the point of us being here?

Mark

There is no point. We're just here to survive for a bit and then we die.

Rox

That's so morbid. When I die, I'll come back and haunt you, then you'll have your proof.

Mark

You know what? I'd love that. I would deliberately live such a boring life just to annoy you. You'll be there desperately trying to haunt me only to have to sit there watching me playing FIFA for five hours straight.

Rox

It might be because I've lost grandparents I loved so much, but I like to hope and believe that they're still around me. I want to think there's still a connection there.

Everyone's looking for something to guide them through this crazy life.

Mark

If believing in ghosts makes somebody feel happier – crack on. I'm all for that. But it doesn't help me and it doesn't make me believe.

Rox

I know loads of people who have had premonitions about something and then it's come true.

Mark

Again, coincidence. I don't believe in fate. I think you make your own luck and your own destiny. You can go after the things you want and achieve them through hard work, drive and commitment. Not through the guidance of ghosts or manifesting it with crystals.

Rox

I'm with you on the last bit.

Mark

I knew you'd come round to my way of thinking.

Rox

Grrrr.

CHRISTMAS: WHEN DOES IT START?

Rox

Christmas begins on 1 November. Mariah gets defrosted, Bublé crawls out of his cave and I put up my decorations.

Mark

This is nonsense, of course. And what makes it even more ridiculous is that I know for a fact you would start even earlier if the children were a bit older.

Rox

Oh yeah, I'd go in September if I could. I only wait until November because I think it would be confusing for the boys to have Hallowe'en in the middle of 'Christmas'. And I'm also aware that other people would think I was totally weird.

Mark

Too late for that, love.

Christmas doesn't start until December. I can get on board with everything festive when we open the first door of the advent calendar. Not a moment before.

Rox

But November's like the pre-match build-up to a football game. It's when the excitement begins.

Mark

Whoa, don't try and win me over by comparing this to football. I'm not falling for that one!

What about Bonfire Night on 5 November? Poor old Guy Fawkes gets no love in our house. Nope, it has to be 1 December and then everything packed away again on New Year's Day.

Rox

That's devastating, Mark. Christmas decs should be up until the end of January.

Mark

It's a new year. Christmas is gone.

Rox

Christmas is more than just a period in time. It's a feeling, it's a spirit.

Mark

Yes, and I do love Christmas when it's actually Christmas. You put me off it by blasting Michael Bublé in the car just because it's 1 November.

Rox

The boys love it!

Mark

Phoenix maybe. Kobe sits there with his headphones on – he knows the score.

And then everywhere we go, the conversation is focused on Christmas. Ooh, I wonder if they've got their Christmas sandwiches out! Oh my god, McDonald's have their Christmas cups! Ah, let's go to the garden centre to see if they've got the singing penguins on display yet!

This is what I deal with.

Rox

It's tradition!

Mark

You can't walk past a hotel without popping in to have a look at their tree.

Rox

I understand that I'm hugely annoying on the Christmas front. But it's my one passion. Christmas is my football.

Mark

Once again, it's nothing like the football, Rox! For two and a half months, every day is an FA Cup Final for you.

Rox

My retirement dream is to set up a Santa's grotto. I want you to grow a beard so you can be Santa.

Mark

Not happening.

Rox

Either that or a Christmas tree farm. Dream jobs. Life goals.

Mark

Send help.

6

A Vegas Bombshell

Mark
As much as we'd made the studio flat in Hendon our little haven, there had come a point when we'd needed to get out. There were only so many times we could stomach the cold showers. And the odd blast of central heating every now and again would be nice.

Rox
As soon as the flat's lease came up, we jumped. We'd both moved jobs and were earning a bit more money so we could afford something slightly bigger.

Mark
We ended up renting a two-bedroom flat in Mill Hill which was on the Northern line and a much quicker journey into work. We were happy there for about four years and certainly never considered buying, mainly because the prospect of owning property in London was so far removed from our financial reality.

Rox
You needed a huge deposit which, on our wages, would have taken us decades to save.

Mark

But then my dad's foster mum died and left me a bit of inheritance, which I hadn't been expecting. And Rox had also been given a lump sum from her dad after her grandad Bill passed away and we suddenly found ourselves with about twenty grand.

Rox

The old me would have blown that on the holiday of a lifetime.

Mark

I reckoned this was the most amount of money we would ever have at once and we should therefore probably look at buying somewhere. It still wasn't nearly enough for a deposit on a place in London and so we started looking further out where properties were cheaper, but there was a quick train line into the capital.

Rox

We used to drive about at weekends searching for potentially affordable areas – we didn't have a clue what we were doing, just winging it as usual. One day, as we were driving from Watford to St Albans, we went through a place I'd never even heard of called Hemel Hempstead and spotted a huge piece of land that was being developed. There were a load of new flats and houses due to be built and so, completely off the cuff, we decided to go and have a nosey. There was a showroom and the lady said the houses wouldn't be ready for a while but some were going to be available to purchase using the government's Help to Buy scheme.

Mark

Help to Buy was set up for first-time buyers like us and meant we only needed to cover 25 per cent of the deposit while the government paid the rest in a shared ownership.

We worked out that we could just about afford the cheapest property on the development if we opted to use the scheme. However, of the three hundred houses being built on this massive new-build estate, only eight of them were these more affordable three-bed townhouse terraces and so competition for them was going to be crazy.

Rox

There was also a deal that meant if you bought off-plan, putting a deposit down before a brick had even been laid, you could get a bit of a discount.

Mark

The more we learned about it, the more we were interested. But there was already a list of about forty people who had registered their interest in these eight houses. As soon as they were released to buy, the saleswoman was going to ring every person on that list and the first eight people who turned up at the site with a £1,000 deposit would secure one of the houses. Literally first come, first served but with no notice whatsoever.

Rox

It sounded like a brutal process, but the plans for the houses on this new estate looked beautiful and we were both having the same thoughts. Hemel was twenty miles north of London with a forty-five minute direct train journey into Euston and it felt like the perfect move for us.

Mark

For the next three months we pursued that house. Like, obsessively. We'd go there at weekends and pop into the showroom on the 'off chance' just to check on the progress and whether they were any closer to being available.

I think the saleswoman got a bit sick of us.

'I said I'd ring you,' she'd sigh.

'Yeah, but we were, um, just passing ...'

Rox

The day she rang us to say that four of the eight townhouse terraces were being released, we were both in a right flap. It was sheer panic.

Mark

We had to come in and give the deposit in person – that was the deal. So, we both left work early, legged it to Euston and got the train straight to Hemel, where we ended up being the second to arrive. We put down a deposit to secure plot number thirty-four and then we were walked over to an empty field.

'It's going to be right about ... here,' said the saleswoman, pointing to a patch of turf.

Rox

It was impossible to imagine that soon our first home would be built exactly where we were standing. I know inheritance comes tinged with sadness, but I was glad we were able to do something positive with the money we'd been given. Something that was going to give us a much more settled and secure future. I knew my grandad would have been proud.

Mark

Now it was just a waiting game for the place to be built and it would turn out to be another six months before it was finished. It had felt like an age, but we eventually moved into Shearwater Road just two days before Christmas in 2014.

Rox

What a buzz! I felt so lucky. I remember the smell of new paint and that tingling excitement holding the front door keys for the first time.

Mark

It felt like we'd made it in life. That's the best way I can describe it. Just a real sense of achievement. We didn't even have any furniture. We'd managed to get a wardrobe for £100 and our bed for £150 from our Mill Hill landlord. But that was all we had.

Rox

On that first night we ordered in a Chinese takeaway and sat on the floor. No sofa, see?

Mark

To help move our stuff, I'd bought a load of blue tote boxes from a bloke on Gumtree who was selling them for two quid each from his garage in north London. Once we'd unpacked them, I stacked them into the shape of a sofa and we put some pillows down on it to make it vaguely comfortable.

Rox

It was easily the most uncomfortable sofa I'd ever sat on, but we were so bloody happy. Mark also fashioned a temporary dinner table and chairs from those boxes, so we got our money's worth out of them!

Mark

We were both earning OK salaries by that time, but we'd put all our cash into the house so there wasn't any spare to go out and buy furniture.

Rox

We lived with pretty much nothing in it for a while until Mark joined the estate's amazing Facebook group.

Mark

We ended up furnishing the whole house thanks to the buying, selling and swapping on that group!

Rox

Nothing in the house matched, but it didn't matter. I loved living there. I loved coming home to our house and to Mark each day after work. They were very peaceful, happy times.

Mark

The only snag about buying a house together was that it instantly gave everyone a green light to ask us when we were going to get married. Rox is three years older than me and so her friends were starting to settle down and have babies. My mates were still living in shared houses, getting drunk every weekend and playing FIFA.

From 2014 onwards it would be, 'When are you two going to put a ring on it?' and I started to feel real pressure. That pressure grew with every wedding we went to as guests because I'd look around the room and all I could think about was how much this thing had cost.

Most of them must have run past ten grand and we were barely able to afford a wedding dress, let alone everything else you needed.

Rox

I wasn't bothered about a Big Day. I knew I wanted to spend the rest of my life with Mark but, as I mentioned earlier, until I met him, I'd assumed I'd never get married. I was never the sort of girl who dreamed of her wedding day, that was just not my vibe.

Mark

Completely aside from all the wedding talk, Rox had wanted to go to Vegas for years. I'd been for a week with my best mate back when I was working full-time in Asda and I'd always rave about what an amazing place it was. I knew Rox would love it because it's like one big party.

I had a relative who worked for Virgin Atlantic and she'd said that if we ever wanted to go to the States, she would see if she could source some cheap seats. I'd told her to let me know if any ever came up for Vegas and we ended up with two seats for a couple of hundred quid each, flying out in May 2015. Boom.

Rox

I was beside myself. Now that we'd settled into the new house, we were able to save up a bit of money and said we'd treat it as a belated thirtieth birthday celebration for me. We booked a room at the cheap and cheerful Planet Hollywood hotel and that was it. We were going to Vegas, baby!

Mark

One night in the run-up to the holiday, we were watching *The Hangover* and Rox started laughing.

'Imagine,' she said, 'if we ended up accidentally drunk and getting married in Vegas. It's exactly the sort of thing we'd do.'

Rox

I reckon Mark had been thinking the same thing, it was just me who'd been the first one to say it out loud.

Mark

And I said, 'Shall we do it?'

Rox

Waaaaaah! That was Mark's proposal, by the way!

Mark

I googled 'How to get married in Vegas' and read that all we had to do was apply online and pick up our marriage licence in person from the Clark County Bureau at least twenty-four hours before the wedding. That sounded straightforward enough. So far, so simple.

Then I found the website for the Little White Wedding Chapel, which is probably the most iconic wedding venue in Vegas, where loads of people had famously married. Michael Jordan, Britney Spears . . .

Rox

. . . Joan Collins, Judy Garland, Frank Sinatra . . .

Mark

By the end of that week, we'd booked the chapel's Michael Jordan Package, which was $500. For that we would get the ceremony itself, two engraved commemorative glasses, a five-rose bouquet for Rox and a buttonhole for me, and they'd supply our witness. It also included a limousine pickup on the morning of the wedding and a photographer taking pictures of us walking into the chapel, so it was really good value. For an extra two hundred quid there was an option for an Elvis impersonator, but we passed on that.

Rox

Before we'd really had time to think about it, everything was booked and paid for and it was happening! It all felt so wild and spontaneous.

I went to Berketex Brides in House of Fraser on Oxford Street to look for a dress. I had no clue what I was looking for, only that it needed to be light and small so it was easily transportable between here and Vegas.

Because this is me we're talking about, I didn't go for the sensible option. The dress I fell in love with was a big, dramatic number with an Italian veil all the way down to the floor. It was only £150 but it was massive, ridiculous and not at all practical. So obviously I bought it.

I also bought two pairs of white sunglasses from Primark so that we could match and I took some silver trainers because I couldn't be walking round Vegas all day in heels.

Mark

One of the optional extras we did take up was paying £50 to have the ceremony live streamed via a webcam. We'd be able to give our friends and families back in the UK a link so they could join us from across the Atlantic on the day.

Rox

Yeah, um, about that . . .

Mark

Although everyone knew we were going on holiday to Vegas, we didn't tell a soul that we were getting married there. Not even our parents.

Rox

Eek.

Mark

There was a lot going on in our families' lives at the time and the thought of getting everyone together was quite traumatic. There are always family politics at weddings, but this felt especially intense.

Rox

Everyone was dealing with their own life challenges and I just wanted to keep the peace and avoid rocking the boat.

Mark

We thought we were doing the right thing.

Rox

It felt like the most stress-free option. I wanted to marry Mark but I didn't want the panic and the worry that would have come with a proper wedding day.

To me, the day itself wasn't ever a big deal. It was just a natural progression of our relationship.

Mark

I think my parents would have tried to stop us getting married in Vegas if they'd known about it.

Rox

I think you're right. That was another reason we just went ahead – so that no one would try and block it or talk us out of it. We thought the best thing would be to phone them all on the day, tell them what we were about to do and then send them the link to the webcam stream.

Mark

When you say it like that, it sounds really blasé. But it made sense to us at the time.

Rox

And by the time we arrived in Vegas, we were too giddy to think about the consequences. On the morning of 8 May, I was focused on what was going to be the best day ever. I went to the salon, where they did my hair and makeup, and all the girls were like, 'It's your special day!', which swept me along.

Mark

I remember Rox came back to the room where I was ironing my shirt and drinking a Bud Light and she went to get changed. When she stepped out of the bathroom and I saw her in her dress, she knocked my socks off. Rox always looks beautiful to me, but this was next level. She looked stunning. I remember her asking me what I thought.

And he said, 'Oh, Rox, you look lovely.'

There were only a few hours before the ceremony and I said we should probably tell our parents now. So we rang home and that's when all hell broke loose.

I don't know what we expected when we FaceTimed our parents to tell them we were getting married in a matter of hours. I suppose I'd naively thought they'd be really excited for us, but that wasn't what happened at all.

Mark

It felt like our big news went down like a sack of s**t. Everyone was so upset with us. My parents saw it almost like a betrayal because it was the first time in my life that I'd done something major that hadn't involved a discussion with them first. Every decision up until that point had been inclusive of them – going to uni, moving to London – and with this I had completely done my own thing.

I was devastated by the reactions. We'd been so carried away with the idea of getting married in Vegas that I don't think we'd stopped to consider how our families would feel about being left in the dark.

Mark

We were both shocked at how people took the news. We'd assumed that everyone would be happy for us, but I can understand now why they were upset.

Rox

I guess it was selfish. We were in love and doing what made us happy. I don't regret our Vegas wedding because it was our dream day, but I do wish to god things had gone down differently.

Now that I have children of my own, I can see how upsetting that must have been for our parents and although we both had our reasons for doing what we did, I'm gutted it caused the family so much sadness.

Mark

I don't know how we could have done it differently and still had the same experience, though. If we'd told people, some of them would have booked flights and flown out to be with us. But that would have caused problems with others who couldn't afford to come. We were screwed whichever way.

Rox

We told them we would have a big party when we got back to make amends for running off, but no one was interested in that and it didn't make them feel any better.

These sorts of problems were exactly what we thought would happen if we'd stayed in the UK to get married. This was what we'd been hoping to avoid.

Mark

We told them we would send over the link so they could join us on the webcam, but apart from that there was nothing more we could do except make the most of the day. Everything was booked, I was in my suit, Rox was in her dress and the limo was on its way. We just had to go for it.

Rox

We had to put all that aside and focus on the day. We each had a Bud Light in the room, Mark put his Forest scarf on under his shirt (you can probably hear the sound of my eyes rolling to the back of my head at that) and we went to get in the limo just as it started to rain. It hadn't rained in Vegas for months and the driver said this was a sign of good luck for us. I said I'd take that!

Mark

The chapel had said they'd supply a witness, but the day before the wedding, I'd noticed on Facebook that two girls who'd worked with me at Asda years ago were travelling around America and had tagged themselves as being in Vegas. I dropped them a message saying we were in Vegas as well and asking if they were free at all the next day. She said they'd not made any plans yet.

'Do you want to come to our wedding?'

'What?'

'Me and Rox are getting married tomorrow, but no one knows. Do you want to come?'

'You're joking!'

'Will you come?'

'Of course, but I've not got anything "weddingy" to wear!'

Rox

Bless them, they both came in their sandals and little dresses and they were our witnesses, which was as lovely as it was random.

Mark

We didn't write any special vows, but it was all very traditional. We'd bought our rings while we were out there – Rox chose an engagement ring at the same time so that was an expensive day out.

Rox

We'd sent the webcam link to all our friends with a text saying something along the lines of, 'Guess what?' I think they thought we were winding them up until they tuned in. And they were all there with us, watching on their laptops and tablets back in the UK, wearing their PJs because they were seven hours ahead.

Mark

They all sent us photos of themselves later and it was so funny.

Rox

At the end of the ceremony, we headed downtown to the Heart Attack Grill. Only in America . . .

Mark

It serves heart-attack food – high-calorie, high-fat hamburgers the size of your head which you can have as many of as you want. You have to dress up in a hospital gown to eat and the deal is if you don't finish it, one of the nurses/waitresses spanks you with a giant wooden paddle in front of the whole restaurant.

Rox

So weird. They weigh you as you leave as well – toxic or what?

Mark

Rox couldn't finish her plate and so she got spanked in her wedding dress with everyone watching.

Rox

It sounds really dodgy when you put it like that. But when you're in that Vegas bubble, anything goes and everything kind of makes sense.

Mark

Then we headed to the zip wire. As you do.

Rox

I went on the SlotZilla Zip Line, still wearing my wedding dress and it takes you right over Old Vegas. People were screaming, 'OHMYGOD YOU GOT MARRIED!' and all I could think of was 'everyone on the ground can definitely see my arse right now ...'

Mark

And then we walked the streets of Vegas, with strangers coming up to us to say congratulations.

Rox

Walking around Vegas in a wedding dress was carnage.

Mark

A group of women came running up to Rox and gave her a handful of dollar bills and told us to get ourselves some drinks. We went to Caesar's Palace and there were some lads at the bar who saw us and were like, 'OK, we're buying *these* people drinks!' It was amazing and we were so up for the party.

We'd also paid a local wedding photographer to come around with us for the day taking pictures and she knew loads of great hidden areas to visit off the beaten track. On her recommendation, we ended up in Old Vegas in this really dark saloon-style pub.

Rox

She'd told us it was the place that did the best tequila, so we knocked back a few of them.

Mark

We were both knackered after that and so we called it a night and went to bed quite early. It had been the best day of both our lives, but at the back of our minds was the knowledge that in about forty-eight hours' time we would have to fly home and face the music.

Rox

And coming back was total drama. No one was happy for us. I went to see my mum in person and she was still very tearful.

Mark

All our friends loved it; they thought it was brilliant and were really supportive. But no one in our families said anything positive. We sent over photographs and the response was so . . . muted.

Rox

A couple of months later, we threw a huge party in the town hall in Hemel Hempstead and made it Vegas-themed. I wore my dress again and we had an Elvis impersonator who danced the night away with my nan – it was lovely to see her enjoying herself and loving life so much because by that point she was losing her sight and was becoming increasingly frail.

All our friends and family came and, overall, it was a lovely evening.

Mark

It took a bit of time for some people to get over it, but we were all able to move on from it even though we felt we were never fully forgiven.

Rox

Whilst maybe we could have done things differently, it's sad that the happiest day of our lives is overshadowed with guilt.

Mark

What surprised me after the wedding was that the constant 'When are you getting married?' chatter immediately switched to 'When are you going to have a baby?'

Whenever we were asked, we kept it vague and just said we'd get round to it at some point, but it wasn't top of the list! Two of Rox's closest friends had just had kids and they were keen to know when we'd be joining them – they both said that getting pregnant could take a little while and we should bear that in mind.

Rox

I'd never been pregnant before and didn't even know whether I'd be able to have children, so it did prey on my mind a little bit. What if we struggled?

Mark

I hadn't actually considered that it might take a long time to get pregnant. We thought about it from the perspective of perhaps wanting a kid in a couple of years' time and so maybe we should start trying now. Ish? Perhaps?

We decided not to 'try' exactly, but to stop being quite as careful.

Rox

And, I swear to god, the first time we 'didn't try' is when it happened. Within a week, I was pregnant.

7

We Are Family

Mark
Not to blow my own trumpet here, but I knew Rox was pregnant even before she did.

Rox
All right, all right, smartarse! It was late July possibly into early August 2015. I was a couple of days late on my period and felt a bit woozy, and it *had* briefly crossed my mind that I *might* be pregnant. But I kept telling myself there was no way I could be. It didn't happen this quick.

Mark
I was convinced, but it was like Rox was in a state of denial.

Rox
Quite apart from anything else, I was due to go on a friend's hen do at Wilderness Festival in Oxfordshire for a big four-day party. This was not the time.

Mark
For the next few days we had the whole 'test or not to test?' chat until she decided that she'd do one if only to rule it out.

Rox

Mark said he thought it might show as positive, but I was adamant it was a false alarm. No, no, no. Definitely not. No chance.

Mark

We had a pack of three tests and sure enough, the first one came back positive. Rox insisted that it must be wrong. She did the other two which both said the same thing. I was ecstatic, but Rox just looked terrified.

Rox

I had to sit on the end of the bed to calm myself down. I needed ventilation, it felt like I was going to have a panic attack. Meanwhile, Mark was jumping around the room going: 'Get in! Yaaaaaaas! I knew it!'

Mark

She said: 'You knew? Why didn't you tell me?' I said I flipping well *had* told her, she just hadn't wanted to hear it.

Rox

There was a lot to take in. Part of me was in shock that I 'worked' properly. I know that sounds odd, but as a woman you never know for certain if you're going to be able to carry a child and I always think you're lucky if you can.

The other dilemma making my head spin was what this would mean for my career. I'd worked so hard to go to uni and get my degree and I was making my way and climbing the ladder as an art director. And now . . . I knew we both wanted a family, but was this too soon?

Don't get me wrong, I was grateful for what was happening, but it was so much quicker than we'd expected. This was a thunderbolt.

And my third thought was, 'What on earth should I do about this hen party?'

Mark

I told her to pull herself together and get to Wilderness. There was nothing to stop her going and still having a fantastic time.

Rox

It was too early to tell people – this was Brand New Information and I hadn't even got my own head round the idea, let alone felt in a position where I could share the news. But how was I going to get through a whole weekend at a boozy festival without anyone realising that I wasn't drinking?

Mark

We came up with a cunning plan and bought a load of non-alcoholic cider which we poured into an empty two-litre bottle of alcoholic cider and Rox took that with her and hoped that no one would twig.

Rox

I hated that bloody cider, it was rank. My friends were all asking why I wouldn't join them on the Prosecco, but I managed to make my excuses and they didn't hassle me after that. Maybe there was some female intuition at play – they'd secretly cottoned on and decided to drop it.

I actually had a really nice time and danced all night to Björk and Roísín Murphy, but being stone-cold sober while everyone else was hammered was an interesting experience. And I couldn't let my hair down completely because I was still very scared. I'd just found out this huge news, the biggest thing that was ever going to happen to me, and yet I couldn't tell anyone.

I was also immediately super protective of my unborn child and felt quite vulnerable at times. I just wanted to make sure

I looked after myself and those feelings were so powerful that they made me realise how much I wanted this baby.

As someone who had been so career-minded and never particularly maternal, that was a revelation to me.

Mark

Those early weeks and months of pregnancy were not easy for Rox, though. We all know that she's dramatic at the best of times – she'll have a mild case of the flu and want to phone for an ambulance. Pregnancy was never going to be a walk in the park.

Rox

It's because I'm usually so happy and high on life, so therefore when I feel bad it's like the end of the world for me! And I really did struggle with the worst nausea. It wasn't morning sickness; it was *all-day* sickness.

Mark

To be fair, you were put through it big time.

Rox

People might judge me for admitting this because I know we're all supposed to be floaty earth mothers, wafting around stroking our baby bumps, but I didn't enjoy pregnancy. Not a bit.

A couple of months in, I was diagnosed with hyperemesis gravidarum, which is the same extreme sickness Kate Middleton had with all her pregnancies, and at one point I was so ill I could barely eat. I already suffered from travel sickness pre-pregnancy, but this was now even worse and I'd throw up travelling any distance. I'd pass out on the train going into work. It was like my body couldn't deal with being pregnant.

Things got so bad that I had to go into hospital, where I was put on an IV drip to get some fluids back into me. After that, they managed to get the sickness under some control with tablets, but it was horrendous. I didn't know how I was going to get through the months ahead.

Mark

In the second trimester, it just disappeared and so there was this middle period where everything was OK.

Rox

But then my hips went. I had symphysis pubis dysfunction (SPD), which meant I was in constant pain around my hips and pelvis. I was like a bowling ball on legs, I was carrying that much water. I just didn't cope well physically or mentally, and I spent a lot of the pregnancy willing it to be over.

Mark

I just wanted to support Rox however I could and one of the ways to do this was to sign up to do a course of NCT antenatal classes together. That was the best thing I ever did because the NCT went on to teach me everything I know about pregnancy, childbirth and babies. I'd known nothing before then.

Rox had a lot of friends around her who were having or who'd had kids and she was reading all the parenting books. She had more of an idea of what lay ahead. I had nothing. And so during every NCT class I'd be sitting there with my mind blown. I was wowed by everything.

Rox

The antenatal teacher got out these charts to show how wide the cervix dilates during labour and Mark blurted out, 'That's the size of a microwaveable Chicago pizza!' That poor woman's face.

Mark

For me, every class was *incredible*. They taught us how to hold a baby, how to change it, how to wind it.

Rox

When Phoenix arrived, Mark was the undisputed world winding champion, so the lessons paid off!

Mark

As dramatic as ever, Rox was 'in labour' four weeks running before it happened for real. In that last month, she was convinced every twinge was the start of labour. How many times were we turned away from the hospital?

Rox

Be fair. I had those Braxton Hicks contractions really bad and when you've not had a baby before, you don't know what labour feels like!

Mark

We knew we were having a boy and every five minutes, she'd suddenly go, 'He's coming!' He never was.

Rox

Until he did. And that was on 1 April 2016. Little Phoenix. Our Nix.

The only birth plan I had was that I wanted an epidural. I was absolutely crystal clear about that. I didn't want the pain or for my baby to be born to the sound of me screaming. I just wanted a tranquil environment. As we've already established, I can be prone to a touch of the dramz and I didn't think I'd be able to push a baby out without pain relief.

Mark

When we arrived on the labour ward, there was a poor woman who was screaming like she was possessed. I've never heard anything like it in my life and I could see that Rox was petrified thinking that was what was coming for her.

I asked the nurse if the woman was OK and she said yes but she'd missed the chance to have an epidural.

Rox

That sent me into a full-blown frenzy. I couldn't miss the chance. Please don't let me miss the chance! Could I order mine in advance?

The nurse said I wasn't far along enough or in enough pain to warrant one just yet, but I knew it sometimes took a long time for the anaesthetist to come and administer it.

'Can I pre-book mine, like now?' I begged the nurse.

I couldn't risk getting to the point of the woman who was screaming her head off. I went on and on so much that eventually I think they gave me it just to shut me up.

Mark

It's a long old process, labour, isn't it? A lot of waiting for the action to start.

Rox

Mark brought a joke book; I kid you not.

Mark

Come on now, Rox. You found those jokes hilarious.

Rox

I do have a weakness for old-fashioned crap jokes.

Mark

Q: What do you call a man with a spade on his head?
A: Dug

Rox

Yep, that one got me.

Mark

Q: What do you call a vicar on a motorbike?

A: Rev.

Rox

Haha! Dying, here!

Mark

So I was reading out these terrible jokes and Rox was howling with laughter.

Rox

The midwife didn't know what the hell was going on.

Mark

The funniest thing was the fact that we'd brought this suitcase which was so full of Rox's favourite snacks that they out-weighed the clothes. But we *hadn't* known that Rox couldn't eat while she was in active labour – when the midwife mentioned it, Rox's face fell.

Waste not, want not. I unzipped the case and got out a four-pack of Snickers and cracked them open while Rox gave me evils.

Rox

He was saying, 'Mmm, these are the best Snickers I've ever had' and I could have killed him.

Mark

I wasn't even hungry.

Rox

As a matter of fact, I could have killed him a number of times throughout labour. Remember your nap?

Mark

Let me explain that one. There was a period where Rox had been less than nice to me and bear in mind that I hadn't slept in what felt like an eternity.

Rox

The state of this ...

Mark

I was exhausted from being a constant, unwavering rock of support to Rox ...

Rox

Jeeez.

Mark

... and I remember the midwife walking in to take some blood-pressure readings while I was sitting on this plastic chair struggling to keep my eyes open. She took one look at me and then turned to Rox and said, 'Let him sleep, baby girl.' And I was just like, 'Thank you so much.'

Rox

And here's me, lost for words.

She said: 'You've got to leave him alone. Daddy needs his rest.'

Mark

And so, following my *instructions* from the midwife, I shuffled the chair over to the window, slumped down, rested my weary head against the wall, closed my eyes and went to sleep.

Rox

To actual sleep.

Mark

I must have only had about half an hour, but when I woke up, Rox had her eyes fixed on me.

It was freaky.

'H-h-have you been staring at me the whole time?' I asked.

Rox

Yes. Yes, I had.

I've got to say, though, that midwife was a total diamond and we both thought she was hilarious. The three of us were joking all the way through and we were disappointed that she wasn't on duty when we had Kobe there two years later.

Mark

She was amazing and she got our sense of humour. Because Phoenix was born on April Fool's Day, when he came out, she said, 'Congratulations, it's a baby girl!'

Rox

For a split second she had me!

After a tough pregnancy, the labour had ended up being pretty straightforward. With both Phoenix and then Kobe in 2018, it was twelve hours of labouring and then pushing them out in ten minutes. I didn't want Mark seeing the baby before me and so he stayed with me at the top end.

Mark

Which was fine by me, great idea.

Rox

We'd decided on the name Phoenix way ahead of the birth. We both wanted something that felt very modern and so we started watching futuristic films from the eighties and nineties like *Total Recall* and *Demolition Man* to see what Hollywood thought names in the future would be.

Mark

In *Demolition Man* the lead baddie played by Wesley Snipes is called Simon Phoenix. Obviously Simon wasn't an option (it lacked the pizzazz we were going for) but Phoenix on the other hand . . . it sounded like such a cool name.

Rox

And the minute he was born, I felt we grew up. Seeing that beautiful, perfect little baby for the first time, I immediately felt like I was meant to be a mum. He was only 6lbs 8oz, so tiny that he fitted into the palms of Mark's hands.

I just instinctively knew that, whatever happened, everything would be OK. It's hard to explain but it was like nothing had ever felt quite right until I met Nix. I felt healed from everything bad that had ever happened to me.

Mark

Do you remember the first thing you said to both the boys when you held them for the first time? It was the same for each of them.

Rox

Oh, yeah. I said, 'Happy birthday, baby.' I'd forgotten that.

Mark

I loved him with all my heart but terror was my overriding emotion. He was so delicate and I wasn't confident how to hold him properly. He wasn't the doll we'd passed around at NCT. Now it was real.

Rox

Mark had to leave the ward that evening because they didn't allow dads to stay overnight, and that was a very strange feeling. I was on my own. I watched baby Nix in the Perspex crib until he fell asleep. And then I continued watching him to make sure he didn't stop breathing.

Mark

I drove home in a bit of a daze. I stopped off at McDonald's, bought myself a Big Mac and went back to the house, which felt so still and silent.

Rox

I'd given him a shopping list of urgent essentials.

Mark

As well as Tiny Baby clothes, Rox wanted a rubber ring to sit on post-labour (don't ask), nipple pads, maternity pads and a load of other things that I knew nothing about. This wasn't popping to the shops for a pint of milk and loaf of bread, I was way out of my comfort zone. One of the shop assistants spotted me clutching my list and looking like a rabbit in headlights and she asked if I was OK.

'Ah, are you a new dad? Oh, bless you. Do you want to sit down here and give me your list and I'll get it all for you?'

Rox

You jammy sod!

Mark

A lovely woman, she was. I arrived at the hospital about an hour later, laden down with bags like a total hero.

Rox

That morning, the nurses thought Phoenix was looking a bit jaundiced and they wanted to monitor him. They took him away to a special unit to place him under the lamps and kept an eye on the bilirubin levels in his blood. Although he was only gone for a short while, it felt like an eternity. As a new mum, that separation was gut-wrenching for me.

Mark

It was the first experience of parental worry – something that never goes away, no matter how old they get. Thankfully, he rallied quickly and we were able to be discharged to go home later that day. And that's when the fun and games really began.

Rox

That's one way to describe it, babe!

My milk came in great and Nix was breastfeeding quite well every two or three hours, which I was really pleased about, but he wouldn't settle anywhere other than on me. I would put him on my chest because that was the only place he would calm and then I'd sit up in the bed all night, not daring to move from that position. I knew about the dangers of falling asleep in bed with a baby – I'd read all the books – and I was scared. But unless he was on my chest where he could hear my heartbeat, he would cry and cry and cry.

Mark

He never wanted to be put down and he only ever wanted Rox.

Rox

Mark was brilliant, running around getting me whatever I needed because for most of the day and night I was either feeding Nix or holding him while he slept.

We got a sling and that was a game-changer because it meant I could keep him close to me, but I was also able to get up and about and wasn't so restricted. I'd advise any new parents of a clingy baby to get a carrier – not just for when you're out, but for around the house as well.

Mark
That definitely helped, but we were both anxious first-time parents.

Rox
The health visitor would come and Phoenix was hitting all the right milestones with his growth and tracking his percentile line but even with that reassurance, I was never sure we were doing it right. He seemed constantly hungry, never satisfied and he also developed reflux which made him very uncomfortable and even more unsettled.

Mark
Me and Rox became like passing ships for a while. I'd get back from work at about 6 p.m., we'd grab a bit of dinner and then Rox would go to bed at about seven to try and catch up on sleep. I would take over looking after Phoenix until around midnight or 1 a.m.

Rox
And then I would do the 'through the night' shift.

We became more of a unit. I know a lot of couples find that those early months with all the sleep deprivation puts pressure on their relationship, but it was never like that for us. We weren't individuals any more; we were a team.

Mark

What impacted me also impacted Rox and vice versa, so we had to work together. I think we'd always done that to an extent but now it was more important than ever. There was nothing that couldn't be resolved if we did it together.

Rox

Gosh, just looking back over that time is making me really emotional. Kobe was such a different baby two years later, wasn't he?

Mark

Or maybe we were different parents by then.

Rox

I guess.

Kobe was born on 29 May 2018, weighing 7lbs 8oz so he was a whole pound heavier and he was very serene from the start. He would be quite happy to sit there and watch the world go by – Nix would never have done that. Kobe brought me back to a calmer state and I didn't find it nearly as hard the second time around.

Mark

I think a lot of that came from confidence, though. With a second baby, you know what you're doing, you don't panic as much and you also know that whatever is happening, it's only a phase. Everything we'd learned with Phoenix, we could put into practice with Kobe.

Rox

It was definitely a happier and more relaxed experience as a second-time mum. I'd been convinced Kobe was a girl, though. It was just a very different pregnancy – I didn't have any of the sickness I'd suffered with Phoenix and the cravings were insane. I just wanted apple juice with Kobe, and I drank *gallons* of the stuff!

Mark

We found out the sex at twenty weeks and did a gender reveal video, but up until then we'd only had girls' names.

Rox

I loved Red for a girl. Once I'd got over the shock that we were having another boy (which we were both delighted about, by the way!), we settled on Max as the name. But when Kobe was born he didn't look like a Max. He looked like a Kobe. We both loved the name Kobe (like Kobe Bryant, the late American basketball player).

Mark

The thing is, when you've named your first son Phoenix, you can't call the next one Dave.

Rox

Kobe worked. But after that, I never felt like I wanted a third. Two was cool.

Mark

You know, I always thought you'd want to go again.

Rox

No, mate. I never wanted to go through another labour because I didn't think my body would recover from it. Giving birth is the most unnatural thing in the world.

Mark

Um, Rox, it's probably the *exact* opposite of that.

Rox

OK, on paper maybe. But I think most women will understand what I'm saying here. I didn't think my physical and mental capacity could take it again. Everyone would say to me, 'Don't you want to try for a girl?'

Nope!

I've never thought that. I was enormously lucky to have my beautiful boys and I felt done. It was like, 'OK, let's all go on an adventure now'.

Our family was complete.

Mark

The whole time we'd been together, Rox had always earned a lot more than me. She was older and so had a three-year head start in terms of her career; she was an art director and they were paid more than designers, and she'd worked at bigger and better agencies.

She'd been freelance for the three years before we had Phoenix, so we didn't have the security of paid maternity leave, but we'd managed to save a fair bit to cover her time off.

Rox

However, following Phoenix's birth and that first maternity leave, the drop down to a single income was tough. We had to be so careful with our money, and budget like hell. Our families helped us out with various bits of baby equipment – Mark's mum and dad bought us the buggy and my nan bought us the car seat, but we had to seriously tighten our belts.

Mark

It was probably about six months in that we really started to struggle. The reserve we'd saved up while Rox had still been working was now empty and we had to sit down and really look at how we were going to survive on my wage alone.

Rox

One of the options was me returning to work, but I wasn't anywhere near ready. I wanted to stay with my baby, who needed me. I also knew we wouldn't have been able to afford childcare. Once we'd factored in the cost of a nursery place and the travel into London, I'd have barely been left with anything from my salary and for what? I'd hardly ever see my child.

Mark

We worked out a plan. Once the mortgage had gone out, the gas and electric and other essentials like my travelcard, we would withdraw what was left from the bank in cash and divvy it up for the four weeks until my next pay day.

Rox

We kept the cash on a little gold tray in the hallway and it worked out that we had £20 a week for groceries which, as you can imagine, didn't go very far at all.

Mark

The place where I worked at the time had free loaves of bread so you could get yourself some toast for breakfast. I used to go into the office, have my toast and then squirrel some extra slices of the bread away in my drawer so I could use them to make a sandwich at lunch. I'd buy a pack of ham from Tesco which I'd keep in the work fridge and it would last me the week. Anything to save a bit of money.

Rox

We didn't tell people how much we were struggling because we were so embarrassed. I'd been this hotshot London career girl, but now I was worried about putting food on the table. I hated having to rely on Mark's salary and it felt like I'd failed.

Yes, we had a roof over our heads, our baby was happy and he was being fed, but I hated living with this financial anxiety.

And I missed Mark. He'd taken a new job purely because it was a tiny bit more money, but it meant he was getting up and leaving the house at a horrible hour of the morning and we never saw each other.

Mark

And I still wasn't earning enough to touch the sides of the loss of Rox's wage.

Rox

I couldn't afford to take Phoenix to baby yoga or sensory classes, so I would try and find free things to fill our days. We spent a lot of time out walking and there was a weekly group at our local church, which was a bit of a lifeline. The days were long, though. I missed adult interaction and I definitely felt lonely.

Mark

There was one day when things reached breaking point. Rox has spoken about this before and it's not something we're going to shy away from because it had such a profound effect on us both and would go on to inform our work with the Trussell Trust.

Rox

Monday was food shop day and I'd take the twenty quid cash from the gold tray and walk to the bottom of the hill to Aldi to get the weekly groceries.

I'd have my list of essentials like nappies, wipes and baby formula. I'd breastfed for as long as I could, but had moved to formula when Nix was a few months old. Me and Mark were fine on pasta, bread and milk. I didn't care what we ate as long as the baby was OK.

So, that day I got everything in my basket, queued up at the checkout and then rang it all through. I thought I'd calculated correctly so it would be within the £20 budget, but it was 70p over. I didn't have that. I only had my £20 note.

I started to panic, wondering what I could put back to bring the total down. We needed nappies, wipes and formula. The only thing was the pasta. Fine, me and Mark wouldn't eat.

And then this guy behind me, who must have seen me getting flustered, came over to me and gave me a pound.

I said, 'Oh no, no, it's fine, honestly.' I was so embarrassed that it had come to this.

And he said, 'Please just take it, it's not a problem.'

I thanked him, almost in tears by now. He wouldn't even accept the change. And I came out of that shop an absolute wreck.

Mark

Rox phoned me up to tell me what had happened and she couldn't get her words out for crying.

Rox

I was absolutely mortified. Even though it wasn't my fault and I do know that now, it felt like it was. I had this beautiful baby and what sort of life was this for him? I couldn't even afford to buy him a new pair of fricking socks. This wasn't fair. This wasn't how it was supposed to be.

I walked home, pushing the buggy up that stupid hill, crying my eyes out thinking, 'This is s**t.' How had my life become this? I couldn't believe this was happening and I felt so ashamed and crushed by this sadness and feelings of failure.

When I got home, I just sat on the sofa with Phoenix and cried and cried.

Mark called to check in on me and in typical fashion he managed to crack a joke which made me laugh. But it was honestly a moment in my life I will never forget.

I still couldn't tell anyone – not my friends, not my family – because of the shame. My mum was already helping us out with bits of cash every now and again; I didn't want her to know how bad things were.

Mark

We hid it well. To the outside we probably looked like we were managing, although we never bought new things.

Rox

Mark wore the same pair of Asda jeans for six years.

Mark

I was constantly applying for new jobs, hoping that one would land, but it was desperate.

I saw that the Sainsbury's in Hemel Hempstead was looking for evening drivers for home-shopping deliveries and I told Rox I was going to apply. If I could leave the office in London bang on time, I could make it back to start a Sainsbury's shift and do a few hours of delivery driving.

Rox

I didn't want him to do it; I thought he'd be running himself into the ground. But we didn't have any other options.

Mark

At that critical point, an old friend of Rox's offered me a new job and a pay rise. It was a stroke of luck and perfect timing, which eased things financially and meant I didn't have to go for the second job at Sainsbury's.

And there was also something else bubbling away in the

background. A Facebook blog that I'd started soon after Phoenix was born was starting to gain some traction.

If I could just work out how to capitalise on that interest, perhaps it would turn out to be a useful little side earner.

Who knew?

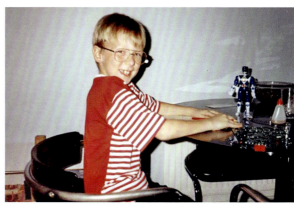

Mark at home in Nottingham sporting his super-fashionable glasses while playing with his Power Rangers.

Here's mini Mark looking very dapper in his little tank top! We think he looks so much like Kobe here.

Rox with her sis and grandad Bill – the most cockney cockney you could ever have met!

Will she be on Santa's nice or naughty list? Rox looking full of mischief at Christmas 1986.

This is Rox's least favourite photo of herself ever. So OBVIOUSLY we had to get it in the book. Haha!

The look of love?! January 2011 and the night we met in Jerusalem, London's 'premier' nightspot . . .

This was our first Nottingham Forest game together and I got Rox wearing a Forest scarf. True love!

This was our tiny one-room flat in Hendon. Hard to believe this is where we once lived. Here's Mark sitting on our bed/wardrobe.

As you can see, there was a beautiful view from the room! We didn't even have an oven to cook dinners, but we both have such happy memories of living here.

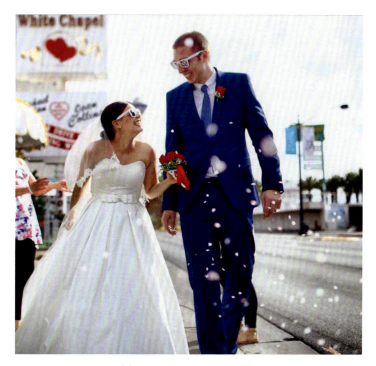

Our Vegas wedding in 2015. We had the best day ever
and made memories that will last a lifetime.

Beat that for a wedding breakfast! Tucking into
our feast at the Heart Attack Grill.

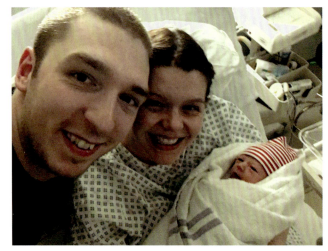

And there he is. Baby Phoenix, born 1 April 2016.

Thumbs up if you're about to have your worlds turned upside down as first-time parents! Gulp!

Such a cutie! It's actually hard to remember Nix being this little.

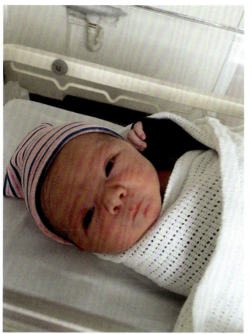

Baby Kobe. Born 29 May 2018.
Our family is complete.

We named Kobe after Kobe Bryant,
the late American basketball player, after
falling in love with the name.

Kobe enjoying skin-to-skin with Rox.

Dressed up to the nines in our sausage roll outfits, on our way to the Brit Awards in 2020. We thought we were going as VIPs . . . but it didn't quite work out that way.

The famous car-wrap prank in 2018. Look at how pleased Rox is with herself!

Winning Celebrity Dad of the Year in 2018. Kobe was just a couple of weeks old here.

Not to be outdone, Rox wins Celebrity Mum of the Year in 2019!

We did it! Celebrating our first Christmas number one in 2018 with the boys.

Recording what would be the second Christmas number one at the world-famous Abbey Road Studios in 2019. We dressed the part this time!

God bless Ronan Keating! Here we are at the studio in 2020 recording song number three.

Possibly the most nerve-racking meeting of our lives. At a hotel in 2021 with Ed Sheeran, sharing the lyrics we'd written with him for the first time.

Sir Elton! What a legend. Spending the day with him is something we'll treasure for ever.

Five Christmas number ones! We honestly still pinch ourselves. Thank you to everyone who helped make it happen for the Trussell Trust.

Rox's favourite time of year. This is us on Christmas Day 2021, the first Christmas in our new house.

8

The Birth of LadBaby

Mark

Believe it or not, LadBaby was initially born out of me wanting to make some dad friends. As we'd got closer to the birth of Phoenix, it had dawned on me that I had no idea *at all* what it meant to become a father and I was looking for a bit of support and companionship from people who were in the same boat. None of my mates were dads (still too busy playing FIFA in their bedrooms) so I had no points of reference and, although I tried to read the books Rox had bought, my dyslexia meant I struggled to concentrate. Big books aren't how I consume information.

Rox recommended some of the mummy bloggers she liked and they were amazing, but their content was, understandably, female-focused and there wasn't an awful lot I could relate to.

Rox

During my pregnancy, I'd started following a lot of mums on social media. People like Giovanna Fletcher, who I've since become friends with, and other women who were blogging about motherhood on Facebook and Instagram.

Mark

The only thing I looked at on social media was the goals from that weekend's football matches. I had an account on Twitter, but only used it for football news, and I had Instagram, which I'd posted a grand total of three photos to.

When I'd started seeking out parenting content, I realised there were hardly any dad bloggers and the few who *were* out there tended to be what I felt were very middle class and London-centric. Where were the normal, everyday dads doing normal everyday dad things?

Where was the bloke called Dave who runs a chippy and has three kids? Because Dave was the bloke I wanted to follow.

Rox

Mark told me that since no one else was doing it, he'd decided to start a blog himself. The original idea was that he'd take a picture of me and the bump every day for the rest of the pregnancy and post it alongside an extended caption on a Facebook page he'd set up. It would document the preparation and mix of emotions as we approached the birth.

Mark

I'd hoped that it could help me make some dad mates even if they were just online. Blokes who were all going through a similar experience and who could support each other in becoming parents.

I'd also thought, if we were lucky, we might get a few free nappies from it. I'd seen the mum bloggers being sent gifts from Pampers and reckoned it would be a nice perk which would save us a bit of money. Dad friends and nappies, that was literally the extent of my ambition for the blog!

Oh, and I'd decided to call it LadBaby. I was a lad who was having a baby. It wasn't any deeper than that!

Rox

A lot of people don't realise that the LadBaby logo, which Mark designed, is my baby bump in profile. If you look, it's an L and a B merged into one and the B represents a pregnant me. I love it.

Mark

The name itself seemed to work well. At the time, LADbible and UNILAD were huge and their pages were doing really well on Facebook, so 'LadBaby' fitted in with the gist of that.

Rox

There was a bit of a trend at the time to use Facebook to build communities, which is what Mark wanted to do, so it made sense to start it there.

Mark

I already followed a few people who were making videos on Facebook, like Arron Crascall – I used to see his videos go crazy viral and thought he was brilliant. I also liked Man vs Baby. I'm friends with both of them in real life now, which is mad and wonderful.

I'd seen the sort of thing they were doing and liked it. But in terms of creating a space for myself and then growing an audience, I didn't have the first clue. I was making it up as I went along.

Rox

And I wasn't tech savvy, so couldn't really help.

Mark

So right in the beginning, at the start of 2016, it had been a daily photo and that could be Rox in the kitchen at home or us at our NCT class or buying nappies and baby clothes in preparation for the arrival. I'd pull together a caption for every image, which I used to write on my way into work each morning.

After Phoenix was born, I'd write about being a new dad, always trying to find the funnier side of those hardcore early weeks and months. Sometimes I'd share videos and posts from other pages that had made me laugh.

And I did that every day and, over that first year, I amassed about a thousand followers, which wasn't bad, but neither was it going to set the world on fire. In the summer, when Phoenix was about four months old, it suddenly jumped by about five hundred and I remember feeling very conscious that I had fifteen hundred people watching me and I started triple-checking my spelling and grammar to make sure it was all correct.

Rox

Posting something for fifteen hundred followers made Mark more nervous than it does now for several million. It used to take him an age to hit that button to upload anything.

Mark

Because it felt so precarious. One false move could wipe five hundred off your following and when you don't have much more than that in the first place, you're going to feel it. You could easily lose nearly half your audience in one fell swoop.

I'd been plugging away at it for a few months when, in the autumn of 2016, I was nominated for a Mumsnet blogging award for best comic writer (woohoo!) and was invited to the event. I was one of only three blokes at this Mumsnet do and managed to survive unscathed! And although I didn't win it, it felt like a moment.

There was a guy filming it for their socials and he asked me the name of my channel, how long I'd been doing it for and how many followers I had. I explained that the concept was built around this daily photo. He asked if I'd ever thought about doing videos or vlogs, but I was dead against that.

'I'll never do that,' I said. 'You'll never catch me doing videos, I'll just stick to photos.'

I didn't have the confidence for it and I hated the sound of my own voice.

Rox

Mark's voice is very distinctive. And boy, does it carry. He has to whisper to me in supermarkets now because otherwise people will come down from two aisles away having heard and recognised his voice.

And for the most part, he wasn't even in the photos himself. It was mainly me and sometimes he'd be pictured buying something or his face would pop up in the background.

Mark

I was always terribly conscious of smiling because my teeth weren't great and I'd got used to covering them up over the years. I've got an Invisalign aligner now to straighten them out, which is something I've dreamed of having since I was eighteen. But back then, being visible online was never something I wanted to do.

Rox

But it was getting to the point where this blog was taking up so much of Mark's energy and time that I started to question how much longer he was going to do it for. He was commuting into London every day and then coming home and working on this Facebook page that didn't seem to be taking off in the way he'd hoped.

Mark

It was quite disheartening when I'd spend hours crafting a blog post only for it to get three measly likes.

Rox

Some people, even our friends, could be quite spiky about it, couldn't they?

Mark

Yes, there was a fair bit of judginess from people who didn't see the point of it. And I started to wonder if I was wasting my time as well. By now we were into 2017 and it didn't appear to be going anywhere. I hadn't won the Mumsnet award, the follower numbers had plateaued and the ones still there weren't engaging as much as they'd used to. Maybe I should cut my losses and knock it on the head.

I decided I would give it until the summer and then quietly retire LadBaby. It had been a fun experiment.

Rox

We're going to let you in on a secret. The famous toolbox video that launched LadBaby into the stratosphere was going to be Mark's final attempt at making his blog work. It was literally going to be his last post.

Mark

Because I was going to bow out anyway, I'd decided that next time I had an idea for a post, I was going to get over my chronic self-consciousness and do a video. I was going to try it, I had nothing to lose at this stage.

I'd tried to do funny posts, parenting posts, money-saving posts – you name it, but nothing was working. Nothing seemed to be registering with anybody. This would be the last try at something a bit different to see if it would fly.

Rox

It all stemmed from a genuine situation. Mark had taken Phoenix to the playground and, between our house and the park, had somehow managed to lose his little lunchbox.

Mark

So Rox packed me off to Sainsbury's with my tail between my legs to get him a replacement. I started filming my stroll down to the shops, thinking I could perhaps edit this down later into a little story, which was the sort of content people were enjoying back then.

Rox

Even just a few years ago, content was much more story-led, with a beginning, middle and an ending. These days everything is a lot quicker, it's all about retention and you have to instantly grab attention otherwise people scroll on by.

Mark

I arrived at Sainsbury's and went to the aisle with the lunch-boxes, but they were all about fifteen quid, which was a ridiculous price to pay for what was, essentially, a small plastic box. By chance, that same day, Bunnings (a massive hardware store from Australia) had taken over our local Homebase and I decided to pop in and have a look around. Admittedly, I was partly enticed by the free hot dogs they were giving away. 'Sizzling sausages,' it said outside, so I thought I'd have a bit of that.

Anyway, while I was in Bunnings, I spotted these toolboxes for four quid. They had lots of different compartments, which would be ideal for separating snacks. Yes, mate!

Sure, it was basic and wasn't plastered with Paw Patrol or Bluey branding, but Phoenix was only fifteen months. Would he care about that?

It would do the job for a fraction of the cost of the Sainsbury's boxes. Sold.

Rox

I thought he'd finally lost it when he came back with that. He wanted me to walk around town carrying a bloody toolbox. Was he actually joking?

Mark

But you came round, didn't you? I went into the kitchen and filled it with fruit, nuts, cheese and snack bars. I even put a miniature Jack Daniel's in there in case Rox was having a hard day. See? Always thinking.

Rox

I didn't know whether to laugh or cry. I just remember Nix's bemused little face.

Mark

And the best bit was, it was double-sided and so you flipped it over and I'd filled the reverse with toys.

'Tell me this isn't the greatest thing you've ever seen,' I said to Rox.

Rox

I had to admit it was good. Genius, even. He'd won me over.

Mark

I had all the footage on my phone, but I'd never really edited anything like this before, so I was learning on the job. I downloaded a free editing app and sat down that evening to figure it out. It took me about three hours to clip together a six-minute video which I titled 'When Dad Invents the Toolbox Lunchbox' and I uploaded it at 9 p.m.

Rox

Neither of us thought any more about it. I remember we watched *Independence Day*, which is my favourite film, and one I've made Mark watch more times that we can count. And then we went to bed.

Mark

When we got up the following morning, we were dashing out to a kids' birthday party and so I didn't get a chance to check Facebook to see how the video was doing. I didn't routinely do that anyway – I'd got used to putting up posts that didn't get much response.

It wasn't until one of the dads at the party came over to me at the buffet and said he'd really enjoyed my toolbox video that I realised something very strange was happening.

I got a bit embarrassed and I could feel my face going red.

'Thank you,' I said. 'I didn't know you followed me.'

He said he didn't. The video had popped up on his feed and he'd seen it that way.

'Oh, right,' I said. 'I wonder how that's happened.'

'It's had about half a million views,' he said.

'Eh? But I've only got fifteen hundred followers . . .'

'Honestly, mate,' he said, 'have a look.'

So I got my phone out, opened the Facebook app and it was like my phone exploded. Notifications, likes, shares, you name it. It was going insane. I went on to the LadBaby page and every time I refreshed it, the views of the video would jump another ten thousand.

Holy s**t, what was going on?

Rox

I was over on the bouncy castle with Phoenix and I could see Mark in the distance frantically waving at me with a bright red face. I thought he was choking on something!

Mark

I was! Choking with disbelief.

Rox

I clambered off the bouncy castle and as I made my way over, he shouted, 'We have to leave now.'

I said, 'What are you chatting about?'

Mark

I managed to stutter out the immortal line: 'I-I-I think we're going viral.'

Rox

He'd lost me.

'Viral? What do you mean we're going viral?'

I didn't know what the fudge was going on, but Mark's phone was ping-ping-pinging and he was so shocked that he looked like he might keel over. I knew something was kicking off and we were best off saying our goodbyes and going home.

Mark

On the drive back, I tried to work out what on earth could have triggered the avalanche of views. I don't think it was one thing. Obviously, my page was public and anything posted there could be shared right across Facebook. And it was basically the thousand or so people who followed me, sharing it to their own pages or tagging someone who they thought would like it in the comments and then those people doing the same and then the same again. When that happens, it creates this social media snowball.

Rox

People loved it, didn't they? As well as all the shares, there was so much positive feedback coming through on the comments.

They loved the comedy of it but also the brilliant money-saving hack behind it. Over the next day or so, we started getting loads of photos from people to show that they'd gone out and copied the idea for their kids. There must have been a national shortage of toolboxes for a while!

Mark

By the time we got home from the birthday party, which was only a half-hour drive, we'd hit a million views. And then I got a message from a reporter at LADbible asking for permission to share it on their page, which just about finished me off.

Rox

You'd have thought he'd won an Oscar. It was pure, unadulterated joy. Mark had loved LADbible for years and now *they* were wanting to use *his* content. This sort of thing just didn't happen in real life.

Mark

LADbible was the OG viral channel, wasn't it? I couldn't believe this was now where I found myself. Rox was screaming, obviously.

Rox

Can't help myself.

Mark

I was like, 'Oh my god, we've made it!'

Rox

We've got a selfie of that very moment, Mark in his shorts and hat and me hugging the baby, both of us totally bewildered.

Mark

And then our next-door neighbours came over to say they'd seen the video and did we fancy celebrating with them.

Rox

They cracked open the cava, bless them.

Mark

And the whole time, the views were going up and up and up.

Rox

Which was amazing, but also – as you know – completely unprecedented for us. Although we were over the moon, we didn't know what we were going to do with all this attention.

Mark

There's a real misconception about viral videos. I think a lot of people think the money instantly starts rolling in. You've created something that millions of people are watching, so surely you must be making a fortune? Well, not exactly.

I'll tell you how much that toolbox video (currently standing at close to one hundred million views) made us.

One hundred quid.

That's the princely sum LADbible paid me as a gesture of goodwill and for handing over the rights to the video to them. The money didn't matter, though. Now with the clout of LADbible behind it, it was clocking up tens of millions of views.

Rox

We were just happy to see so many people around the world enjoying the video. It did really well in Australia because of the Bunnings connection and it was fantastic to watch this community that Mark had been striving for, finally coming together. Parents like us.

After all this time resisting making videos, it turned out Mark was really good at it and I told him he should keep doing them.

Mark

Having been on the brink of closing the LadBaby page down, I was revitalised. There was a renewed sense of purpose and I resolved that every idea we came up with from this point, we'd share through video because this was clearly the way forward.

But I felt a huge amount of pressure to follow it up. Nobody went viral back-to-back – not newcomers to the scene, anyway. Whatever I did next was going to pale in comparison to what I'd just done. I didn't know how I was going to capitalise on this attention and keep up the momentum.

Rox

The publicity grew the Facebook page but only to about 25,000 followers, which wasn't a huge number considering how many had watched the video.

Mark

I posted a short follow-up called 'Toolbox on Tour', which showed us heading out for the day with the new lunchbox, but it only got around fifty thousand views. A week before this, I'd have been bouncing off the walls with those numbers, but coming straight after the previous one, which had millions (and counting), it was demoralising. It hadn't worked.

I was racking my brains, trying to think of something else we could do and a few days later I did a video where I went back to Bunnings and bought another toolbox, which I said I was going to give away. And that totally flopped.

No one commented, no one liked it. It just sat there, on about ten thousand views, not causing even a minor ripple.

In this industry, you're only ever as successful as your last video. It didn't matter that three days ago I'd produced something that had gone global with crazy views. It felt like I'd gone back to square one.

Rox

I was gutted for Mark. A few days ago, it had been the start of something really exciting, like we were riding the crest of a wave. I wanted Mark to be happy and I could see this was something he really wanted to do. I also knew that it was potentially a one-off. I'm not saying I thought it was a fluke, but I was also trying to be realistic.

Mark

I'd originally thought the Facebook page would grow gradually over the first year, but it hadn't. And then suddenly overnight it was bigger than I ever thought possible. We were in this weird transition period where I wasn't sure where to take it.

Rox

One thing that did come up was an offer from Bunnings to launch an official LadBaby toolbox lunchbox.

Mark

They were keen to make hay while the sun shone and one of the bosses flew in from Australia to meet us. We had a meeting in the café at Bunnings over a hotdog, with their team and someone from a manufacturing company. They asked us to partner with them, which we were really excited about, but there was just one catch. In order to make it compatible with health and safety laws for food, the plastic had to be BPA-free, and that was going to bump the cost up.

Rox

We were so excited. Until they told us they were going to have to charge £14, which defeated the whole object of the hack.

Mark

The point of the video was that I didn't want to pay top whack for a kids' lunchbox and so had found a quick, effective way to cut costs.

We couldn't go ahead. They tried to talk us round and said it was potentially a huge seller, making a lot of money. They even upped the percentage they would pay us from the sales to try and persuade us into an offer we couldn't refuse.

I wasn't bothered about that, though. I would rather turn the money down and go out in a blaze of glory with that amazing video than have everyone say we'd sold our souls.

Rox

We stuck to our guns. And since then we've walked away from countless very lucrative opportunities because of our values. We won't compromise on them or the people who follow us.

Mark

That's what we always come back to. I remember the first Christmas after having Phoenix, Rox bought me a framed dollar bill. Written on the note were the words, 'Do what you love and the money will follow.'

Rox

We've had it in our house ever since and it's something that will always resonate with us. We've never taken a deal because of the money. And companies that we do work with, we always ask if they can give something back – that's how we ended up convincing Pepsi to donate half a million pounds to the Trussell Trust in 2020.

Mark

We once did a talk at a Facebook event where we were on a panel with three other people from the digital world. One of them, who I won't name, told the audience that when someone offers you money, you take it. It shouldn't matter if you don't like the company, or you think what they're asking you to do is a bit s**t, because the game was all about making money and getting paid as much as you can. We were both shocked at how mercenary he was.

Rox

It's not the way we are or ever have been.

Whenever I work with a beauty brand, I put in place stipulations that mean I have to have used the product myself in my everyday life before I promote it. Whether it's a face cream or a lipstick, I will only recommend it if I like it and it actually works. Trust is so important, and the relationship we have with our followers – many of whom have been with us for years – is too special to me to throw away for a cheap buck.

Mark

Not everyone online respects their audience, which is a shame. But I also think people see through that kind of influencer eventually.

Rox

Gosh, we've been to social media events where people have introduced themselves as their follower number. Like, literally, 'Hi, I'm five million.' I always reply, 'OK, and what does your mum call you?' This industry can create monsters.

Mark

Still reeling from the failed attempts to recreate the success of the original toolbox video, I tried various other ideas in the hope that something would stick. I did one called 'How Dads Deal with Dinner Duty', where I ignored Rox's instructions to make Phoenix a healthy meal with pasta and avocado, and took him down to McDonald's for chicken nuggets instead. I put him in his mini car and pushed him through the drive-thru. That one did OK in terms of the numbers, but nothing amazing.

I knew I had to come up with something quickly, otherwise we were going to sink without a trace.

Rox

And that's why, ten days after the toolbox lunchbox, I came home to find a giant pink skip on my driveway.

Mark

Correct. And within the space of a few hours, everything went absolutely crazy again.

9

Skips, Selfies and the Seeds of Success

Rox

People still talk about that skip video all these years later.

Mark

It's one that's stuck in the memory, all right.

Rox

Probably down to the fact that the success of it took us all the way to ITV and *This Morning* with Eamonn and Ruth while Mark froze his tits off on national telly. Not a situation I ever expected to find myself in.

Mark

In case you've not seen it, the idea came from Rox asking me to buy a paddling pool for Phoenix. We were having a rare heatwave in the UK and she wanted somewhere for him to cool down and splash about in.

Well, I quite fancied a cool down and a splash about as well, but obviously I wouldn't fit into a bog-standard paddling pool. I knew I could do better than that and so I phoned a local skip hire company.

Rox

A totally normal thing to do.

Mark

I called up and said I had this Facebook page and wanted to make a film about filling a skip with water and turning it into a swimming pool on the cheap. In a stroke of luck, the woman on the phone had seen our previous videos, loved them and said she would give me the skip for half price. Yes, mate!

I organised for it to be delivered on to our front drive while Rox was out for the day, then I lined it with tarpaulin and filled it with water. When Rox called to say she was on her way back, I put on my trunks and climbed in.

I don't think I've ever been as pleased with myself!

Rox

As I pulled up to the house, there was Mark floating about in this bloody pink skip on a giant inflatable as if he was holidaying in Benidorm. What the . . . ?

'Get me a beer, love!' he called to me.

Mark

Ah, but you were in that skip by the end, weren't you, babe? In your favourite swimmers, a great big smile on your face and winning at life, you were.

Rox

I wouldn't go that far.

Mark

When we put the video out, showing the whole escapade, from the arrival of the skip to Rox taking a dip herself, the response was next level. Unbelievable.

Rox

It reached epic proportions because a few days later, ITV called and it was *This Morning* wanting us to go on the show and recreate the whole bloody thing. Eamonn Holmes and Ruth Langsford were hosting that day and they'd put a skip filled with water in some offensively cold warehouse area of the studios. They billed Mark as 'The Designer Dad' and he was plonked in this skip wearing a T-shirt and trunks. I was there with Phoenix, who was running around and out of control. It was a mad day.

Mark

I could hardly talk to Eamonn and Ruth because I was so cold. If you go and find the interview on YouTube, you'll see my teeth are chattering because this was taking place in the depths of the ITV basement and the water was absolutely baltic.

Rox

We went on a bit of a roll after that, didn't we? We hit a purple patch where everything we put out was doing huge numbers.

Mark

Another video that went down a storm was when the three of us headed to a Nottingham Forest game and Rox managed to blag her way into hospitality with Phoenix. I was in the stand and there she was in the box, giving me the middle finger, living it up like Lady Muck with champagne on tap.

Rox

Anything which told a little story did well and especially if it was a solution (of sorts) to a normal parenting problem. I'd wanted a new baby gate to go across the kitchen doorway because Phoenix was on the move and I needed to keep him contained while I made the dinner. I came home to find Mark claiming to have saved the fifty quid we would have spent on the gate by sawing the kitchen door in half.

Mark
Worked a treat, didn't it?

Rox
What are you on, Mark?!

Mark
I made Phoenix a baby walker out of plumbers' piping with little wheels attached and a bicycle bell.

Rox
To be fair, that was very inventive.

Mark
And it cost less than a tenner!

People also loved the ones where Rox was reacting to me doing something ridiculous. You guys will know that getting a rise out of Rox is what I've always loved to do – she can only respond with drama. She can't do anything else, it's in her DNA.

But really, the only judgement we used when deciding what to post was whether it made us laugh. If it ticked that box, it went up.

Like the time I grew a moustache to go to a friend's wedding.

Rox
It was not a good look, Mark. It felt as if I was married to a Chuckle Brother.

Mark

We made a video about taking the 'tache on tour' to this wedding, which is as daft as it sounds, but it was also really successful.

Rox

Another time we stuck Wotsits to our heads and went for a workout in the gym. As you do.

Mark

That was after over one hundred thousand people on Facebook voted for us to do it. We bought a pair of bald caps, superglued Wotsits to them and headed to the gym.

Rox

We looked a right pair of muppets and we stank of cheese.

Mark

That spin class we did . . .

Rox

Oh, stop it! The absolute hilarity. And you on the treadmill with all the serious bodybuilders looking over with those 'What the actual hell?' expressions on their faces.

Mark

There was no point, but that *was* the point.

It was so much easier to get away with stuff back then because no one knew who we were. Bloody hell, even *I* didn't know who we were or what we were doing! People looked at us like we were mad, but we just carried on regardless in a way that would be impossible today.

Rox

Now we get spotted and someone in authority will tell us to stop filming before we've even had a chance to get started.

Mark

I got banned from a Tesco in Hemel because I filmed without permission. I'd put a basketball net on my back and was going to get the kids to shoot some hoops while I was doing the food shop. The manager came down, stopped everything and told us to leave.

Rox

People sometimes say to me that they miss the old days when we used to make videos in B&M or Poundland. It's because we just can't do that any more. We've not changed, but the situation has.

Mark

Do you remember Madame Tussauds?

Rox

Haha! That was bonkers.

Mark

As a joke, we asked our followers to go on to Madame Tussauds' Facebook account and bombard them with messages saying LadBaby needed their own waxwork in there.

Rox

What a *mental* thing to do. I mean, the confidence was crazy. We were on such a high but thinking it about now, like, what on earth? We didn't really listen to anyone; we just did what we wanted to make the audience smile and that kind of confidence was like a superpower every day. We just believed in ourselves. Neither of us are overly confident people, but we'd found something that made us extremely happy and that meant everything we did was done with joy and positivity.

Mark

We just steamed ahead. We weren't making any money, so we didn't have anything to lose if it all went wrong. So the mind-set was, 'OK, let's just do the weirdest and most fun stuff we can think of' and push it to the max.

I was at work Monday to Friday, but every Saturday I'd film something that I could edit into a story by the Sunday to upload that evening.

Rox

Mark had worked out a timetable, which he stuck to religiously. Every Sunday at 9 p.m., the latest video would go up.

Mark

We were told we were doing it all wrong and that no one posted on a Sunday. It wasn't the done thing.

Rox

But our logic was that at 9 p.m. on a Sunday, everyone is feeling a bit depressed about work the next morning so let's put out something silly to lighten the mood.

Mark

There was never any science behind it, we just went on gut instinct.

Rox

And very quickly, it got to the stage where people were *expecting* it and our followers would be on the page from 8.55 p.m., hitting refresh and waiting for us to post. We used to be able to see how many people were watching it as it went live, which was always mega exciting.

Mark

We've never conformed to social media 'norms' or what other creators are doing.

Rox

We used to get told that we should be filming horizontally like everyone else, but we've always stuck to shooting vertically, figuring that most people would be watching on their mobiles. Vertical fits better on a phone.

Mark

We've had various meetings with YouTube over the years where we've been strongly advised to switch to horizontal, otherwise the algorithms wouldn't pick us up. They've also said we needed to get a better camera, improve the sound and make the films look 'luxurious'. But we thought all those bells and whistles would take away the realness and relatability.

We once sat on a panel with a group of famous YouTubers and they were explaining in great, painstaking, technical detail how they filmed in 4K (which is ultra-high definition) and then resized it for Instagram. When the panel host came to us, we said we just filmed stuff that made us laugh.

Rox

Everyone in that room thought we were stupid.

Mark

When you watch *You've Been Framed*, it doesn't matter how s**t the quality of the home video is: if it's funny, you still laugh, right? If you see somebody falling down a muddy hill, amateurish camerawork doesn't stop it being funny. And that's what

I've always said about our content. From the industry's point of view it really shouldn't have worked, but somehow it did.

Rox

By the second half of 2017, we'd really hit our stride and most of what we were putting out was going crackers. There was the 'When you don't have a babysitter for date night' video, where Mark got an inflatable pub put in the back garden. That's another one that has gone down in LadBaby legend.

Mark

It went nuts. I'd seen a guy advertising this inflatable pub on Facebook and when I got in touch, he drove all the way from Manchester to Hemel Hempstead and lent it to us for free because he'd seen some of our videos and liked them.

Rox

We got stopped for our first ever selfie after that one went out. This random bloke recognised us and said: 'Oh my god, you're the couple who do the videos! Can I get a picture?' Surreal.

Mark

I always love meeting people and would never refuse a photo. I'll never tire of that.

But having a bit of notoriety can also be one of the hazards of the job and has led to some, let's say, interesting encounters. It can be very awkward to be standing at a urinal, doing your business and having someone shout: 'Oh my god! LadBaby's here! Can I get a selfie?'

Rox

I've had girls knocking on the toilet cubicle door while I'm mid-wee. There was one night I had to be helped out of the loos at Popworld by security because there was a *very* merry hen do who were screaming as if it was Celine Dion in the bogs. It was a proper laugh, to be fair, and I was laughing too, but they wouldn't let me go or let me out!

Mark

I was at a football game once and nipped to the loo at half-time. There were about ten blokes at the urinal and right at the end of the line was one who had clearly had a skinful.

'Oh my f***ing god,' he said, 'it's LadBaby!'

Everyone turned and looked at me. This guy had his manhood in one hand and his phone in the other.

'LadBaby, gizza smile!' and he took a picture.

I mean, what can you do?!

Rox

I remember Mark came out of there traumatised.

Mark

The funniest/weirdest/most inappropriate approach for a selfie came when Rox was – wait for it – *in labour.*

Rox

Yep, that one will never be beaten.

Mark

Both our kids were born at Watford General Hospital and we really couldn't fault the care we had there. However, when she was in labour with Kobe, during a lull in between contractions, there was a knock on the door.

Rox

The nurse popped her head in and said, 'I'm so sorry to ask, but there are a few people here who are a bit starstruck. Would you mind if we brought them in to say hi?' Erm . . .

Mark

And about six people – some of them pregnant women, some of them blokes – trooped in and each of them got a selfie with Rox as she lay there on the bed in her hospital gown.

Rox

I'm still speechless about it, if I'm honest. It was very hard not to Karen my own self.

Mark

We didn't know what to do! We were just so astonished, I don't think either of us had the ability to say not today, thank you, she's literally in the middle of having a baby.

Rox

Never let it be said that we ever say no to a selfie.

Mark

By October 2017, we'd hit one million followers on Facebook. LADbible said it was the quickest they'd ever seen any account grow to that level. They were sharing 90 per cent of our videos, which would always send the viewing figures into the millions, but it still never made us any money. We weren't even getting the hundred quid LADbible had used to pay because I'd been advised not to hand them the rights – we should remain the owners of our content.

Rox

It was amazing to see Mark making these short films and people loving them, but we were doing it all for free and it was starting to take up all our spare time. It was hard fitting it in around Mark's work and yet we were also being advised that we weren't posting frequently enough to engage and maintain our audience.

Mark

The team at LADbible said in order to maintain and grow those numbers, I needed to be posting a minimum of every two days, but I physically couldn't do that. I was working long hours in a full-time job with a daily commute and it would have been impossible to be posting any more than I was.

But I always knew it would go somewhere eventually – I just didn't know where or how to get it there.

Rox

Having said all that, it was bringing a lot of fun to our weekends. Those early days were such a laugh.

Mark

What's really strange is that people come up to us now and tell us they've been having a tough time or going through a bit of a moment and they'll watch our videos because the sheer silliness of it all helps them forget about the worries for a while.

What people probably don't realise is those videos got *us* through the early years of parenting when *we* were struggling. Knowing that we had to go and film because people were expecting the latest one to drop on a Sunday evening gave us a real sense of purpose.

Rox

I found a community, too. Phoenix was the kind of kid who never liked to sleep at night. He preferred to party, so he was definitely his mother's son. But it meant I was often awake at unspeakable hours of the morning with a baby refusing to settle. I'd use that time to scroll through the comments and I'd take so much heart from what people were saying about our videos. Sometimes I'd reply at 2 a.m. and get an immediate response because other mums were up at that time, too! The

2 a.m. crew were the best. It felt like we all understood each other and were all in this together.

That sense of solidarity was everything.

Mark

After a few months of being on that roll with the videos, we got our first paid deal in October 2017.

Rox

I'll be forever grateful to Scalextric for that. I can't tell you how much it made me want to cry, the fact that a brand as renowned as that wanted to work with us.

Mark

They paid us two grand for an advert, which felt like we'd won the lottery. We used half of it straight away to pay off the remainder of a loan we'd taken out to cover Rox's maternity.

Rox

It was soooo much money. I remember doing the food shop and thinking, 'Thank the Lord.' It was the first time in so long that I'd been able to go to the supermarket and not have to carefully tot up the contents of the trolley to the exact pence.

And I know that a lot of people won't see what we do as 'hard work'. But for a good few years I'd watched Mark pour his heart and soul into something he believed in. I was just so happy that he was finally getting some reward for all that graft.

Mark

For the advert, I came up with an idea around how to entertain the kids while you were trying to have a meal in a restaurant – a quintessential parenting problem. We filmed it at Pizza Hut in Watford, where the pizza is served on a raised plinth, and we set up the Scalextric track to run around the perimeter of the table. Bingo. That kept Phoenix amused for the time it took me and Rox to eat the food.

Rox

I wanted to take the Scalextric set to every restaurant from then on because it bloody worked. The table next to us thought we were mad, but we filmed it on the iPhone, Mark did the editing and it really was a terrific little ad.

Mark

We were so thrilled to be working with a brand, that we totally over-delivered. They only asked us to put it up on Facebook, but we posted to our Instagram as well and it did really well. We got around fifty thousand likes, nearly twenty thousand shares and seventeen thousand comments, which are good numbers for an advert.

And I thought if we could get one of those deals every six months, it would be a lovely sideline. It would make the work we were putting in worthwhile.

Rox

We also got invited to Whipsnade Zoo for a Rod Campbell event to celebrate the thirty-fifth anniversary of his book *Dear Zoo*. It meant we got into the zoo for FREE and I can't put into words how thrilling this was for me. First Scalextric, now this!

Plus, *actual* Rod Campbell was there reading the *actual* book. I nearly died a death because I had *Dear Zoo* as a kid and it was one I now read to Nix.

Mark

After a while, we felt well established enough to stop sharing the videos with LADbible. They got the views up, but it would also attract comments on the posts like 'this is boring', or 'sick of these two', which were quite annoying and I couldn't be bothered with it any more.

And people were so horrible about my teeth and Rox's weight. We can laugh about that now, but at the time the personal remarks really got to us. So, we took the decision to keep the videos solely for our page where people were there because they liked us and our content and they wanted to be there. We had built such a strong and supportive community there and it felt like we were all on the same wavelength.

Rox

It's why we decided to announce my second pregnancy to our followers. And where else to do it but at Disney?

Mark

I can think of literally a million other places.

Rox

We'd gone to Disneyland Paris for New Year and thought that would be a great time to share the news. At the end of the video we'd made documenting the trip, we did the big reveal, which was me lifting my top up to show the words 'Yes Maaaate' written on my belly in red lipstick.

Mark

It marked the end of what had been a rollercoaster year. I had a feeling 2018 was going to be even bigger.

Shall we talk about your infamous Valentine's Day prank?

Rox

In my defence . . .

Mark

There is no legitimate defence, Roxanne.

Rox

In my defence, I was never bothered about cars. A car is a car is a car to me. I had a white second-hand Nissan Micra that Mark christened the Nan Wagon and all that mattered to me was it got me from A to B in one piece. I didn't realise that a lot of people see their car as their baby. Or an extension of themselves.

Mark

Neither of us had ever had new cars. We'd always had second-hand runarounds that were on their last legs.

Rox

So when I thought up a prank on Mark's Nissan Qashqai, it wasn't a big deal to me.

I rang this car vinyl wrap guy – Sam he was called – and I put my vision to him.

Mark

Your *vision*.

Rox

Yes. I could picture it in my head. I said I wanted him to cover the entirety of my husband's car in vinyl stickers.

'Sure,' he said. 'What did you have in mind?'

'Giant hearts. And I want my face in the hearts.'

'Er, what?'

Even at that point I didn't twig that this was completely mental. Sam agreed to do it and then it was a case of getting the car to him without Mark realising. I only had a small window of time to get it done, but I knew there was a football match Mark was going to and he always went for a drink after the game.

As soon as he left the house, I drove the car round to Sam who did the quickest job of his life. When I went to pick it up and saw it for the first time, I nearly wet myself laughing. I was *dying*. The hearts had come out a lot bigger than I intended . . .

Mark
You don't say.

Rox

But it was perfect. I was so bloody proud of myself! It had 'I love my wife' and 'Happy wife, happy life' adorning the sides and the bonnet, and I honestly thought this was the funniest thing I'd ever done. I reckoned Mark would find it hilarious, too.

Mark
Rox, you'd stuck your face all over my car and it was impossible to get off. In what universe did you think I'd find it hilarious?

Rox

I knew Mark's walk back from the football would go past this car park, so I drove the now-wrapped car there and sat in wait. He's so tall, I could see the top of his head over the wall as he walked past. I shouted over to him, he turned around, saw me and the car and could not compute what was in front of him.

Mark
Well, obviously! Has anyone ever seen anything like that? It was just so *confusing* to me. I kept asking what you'd done. And then walking round the car and seeing that you'd literally covered the whole vehicle, including the roof, which had 'This car is being tracked by my wife' emblazoned across it.

And it was permanent. It wasn't like you'd had a little joke which would be a bit irritating to sort out. The car was going to have to stay like that. I was in shock, mate.

Rox

I didn't realise that it was that extreme until Mark's face stayed in the 'jaw-drop' position. That's when I started to get a bit nervous that maybe I'd taken it too far.

Mark

I had no words. And that doesn't happen very often.

'Happy Valentine's Day,' she said. 'What could say "I love you" more than a giant picture of your favourite person on the planet?'

Rox

When we put the video online it caused a huge reaction and an even bigger divide. All the blokes were like, 'If my missus did this to me, it would be over.' The men absolutely hated me.

The women, however, were cheering me on – it was a husband/wife split down the middle and it was giving me life.

Mark

For about a week I was far too embarrassed to go out in it, but I had no choice – I had to use the car eventually. And when I did, I couldn't go anywhere without being honked at.

Rox

In fairness to the horn beepers, I did have 'honk if you love my wife' on there. They were only doing as they'd been asked.

Do you remember I made page three of the *Nottingham Post*? A big day in the Hoyle household, that was.

Mark

Everywhere I went, people would be laughing and pointing at the car and, as the days passed, I had to laugh with them otherwise I was going to be angry for ever. If you can't beat 'em, join 'em. I ended up driving it for years, until it finally broke down beyond repair. The flippin' stickers outlived the car itself.

Rox

As the video spread like wildfire across the internet, that car became famous. We'd pop out for bread and milk and come back to find people having a selfie with it.

Looking back, it was brash and bold but I didn't think anything beyond, 'Oh, this is well funny and it'll make him laugh.' I didn't really consider the fact he would then have to drive around in it. Neither of us really thought about the consequences.

Mark

And about a week later, in an act of revenge, I got Sam the wrap guy to do the same to Rox's car with my giant face eating a sausage roll. 'My husband is a legend' was written across one side and 'My husband is bigger than yours' along the other. And so then we both had these absurd cars covered in each other's faces.

Rox

Over one hundred million people watched that Valentine's video.

Mark

I don't think we fully comprehended how many people were watching.

Rox

Our videos have had billions of views now. But when you're in the realms of numbers like that, how can you possibly make sense of it?

Mark

When we did our live shows at Christmas in 2023, there were two thousand people in the audience and I was *more* nervous about that because we could see people's faces and how they were reacting. It was much more intimate.

Rox

If we thought about how many people were watching me dancing about like a nutcase on a video, then it would be too much. We have to compartmentalise it otherwise we'd completely lose the plot.

Mark

Did we not lose the plot years ago, anyway?

Rox

Good point.

Mark

In June 2018, I was sitting at my desk at work when an email from the *Daily Mirror* dropped into my inbox. The reporter was asking me for a comment about my nomination for Celebrity Dad of the Year. Er, hello?

That was the first I'd heard of it. I did a bit of googling and it came up on the Sky News website that I was one of the contenders for that year's award.

They had pictures of all the nominees – Simon Cowell looking dapper on a red carpet, Rio Ferdinand holding up the

Champions League trophy, Anthony Joshua with his god-like physique, Prince William being all regal.

And right at the bottom of the page, wearing an ill-fitting shirt, sitting in McDonald's, was yours truly.

Rox

That still makes me laugh. They stitched you right up with that picture!

Mark

Anyway, it was a complete surprise and I was really touched. It was a bit of recognition outside of the social media bubble. Obviously I wasn't a 'celebrity', but it felt like validation, as if something a bit bigger was starting to happen.

I phoned our manager at the time and he said not to get my hopes up.

'Don't get my hopes up? This is massive! My hopes are sky bloody high!'

'Come on now,' he said, 'you're not going to win it. Let's just manage expectations here.'

Rox

Our manager was always such a *positive* presence. I'm joking, by the way.

'Manage expectations' – we heard that a lot. We wanted to push LadBaby to the next level and he would tell us we were overreaching.

Mark

Look, there was no way I should have been on that list, going up against that calibre of people. I was well aware of that. But somehow, I was there and so surely now we had to be positive about it and aim to win? It was down to a public vote – there was everything to play for.

Rox

There were so many people who followed us, loved what Mark was doing and wanted him to fly, so we thought that we must have a chance.

Mark

We started a bit of an election-style campaign to get people to vote for me. I designed a poster mocking up the iconic 2008 Barack Obama 'Hope' image with my face.

Rox

Hope? Classic Mark!

Mark

People really got behind us, but when I found out I'd actually won, I thought it was Rox on the wind-up. They called and told me I'd come top of the poll with more than a quarter of a million votes, which was the most that had ever been registered for a single nominee. It had been a landslide.

Rox

Clas Ohlson, the homeware chain, were the sponsors of the award and we were asked to go to their store in Manchester's Arndale Centre to collect it. Kobe was just two weeks old at this point, so we brought my mum along to help with the boys.

Mark

They'd said to get to the store for a photo shoot but, if I'm honest, it felt like they were disappointed that it wasn't a 'celebrity' who had won. I don't know what I was expecting when we got there, perhaps a few balloons and a bit of a buzz? But when we arrived, it was like they hadn't known we were coming at all.

I walked into the hardware store and went up to an assistant and said I was here for the Celebrity Dad of the Year photo shoot.

'Oh right,' she said, 'I'll just speak to the manager.'

And then someone came up from the warehouse and they suggested we went outside the shop where they took about five pictures and then said thanks for coming.

Rox

That was it. To us it was a really big moment, but because Mark was seen as 'just a YouTuber', it kind of got ignored.

Mark

It was a bit of a let-down to be honest. But we've learned over the years that one thing can turn out to be a stepping stone to something else, and often when you least expect it. Even the setbacks are part of the journey.

And it was around this time that we received what, at first glance, looked like a scam email. It claimed to be from Facebook HQ in California and they said they wanted to talk to us about getting us on board some exciting new program the platform was about to launch.

Rox

It had all the hallmarks of one of those 'Congratulations, you've just won a million pounds! Fill in your bank details below!' type of messages.

Mark

However, the email address it came from seemed legit, so I tentatively replied, hedging our bets but saying we would be interested in hearing more. I got a very quick reply from a guy called Kai who arranged a phone meeting for the next day. Our manager was away on holiday and so I decided I would take the call on my own.

Best phone call ever.

Mark

And here's the thing. Even though the Celebrity Dad of the Year experience turned out to be a bit of a downer, the win itself helped our confidence. We knew we had people behind us – our followers – who believed in us and we were so buoyed by that support.

I reckon that boost gave Mark the belief that he could take the call himself and manage it.

Mark

Totally. Winning that award confirmed that we had a dedicated audience, an army of people who had our backs. I took a lot of heart from that.

Rox

Kai from Facebook called the next day. 'Hi,' he said, 'I'm Kai.' All smooth, he was.

Mark

'Hello?' I answered the call. 'Yes, it's Mark and Roxanne Hoyle, here.'

Rox

We did our best phone voices, didn't we? Trying to be all professional and businesslike. Which was a bit pointless because obviously Kai would have seen us online being absolute doughnuts and known exactly what we were about.

Mark

Facebook was trialling a scheme that would put adverts into videos. So, for instance, if we had a three-minute video, they would place an ad at the start, middle or the end. There were already a few creators based in the States who were trying this out and Kai was asking if we wanted to join them.

Rox

We thought it sounded really interesting. We weren't making any money from our channel as it was and so we felt we might as well go for it.

Mark

It was literally the click of a button. Facebook did something at their end and from that moment, our videos would have adverts.

Rox

We were the guinea pigs. And because we were part of this small group of creators, we got a lot of support from Facebook, who were invested in it being successful.

Mark

We agreed to go ahead, but the first month was chaos. Our videos now had ads, but the views were tanking. The algorithm was all over the place and people just weren't seeing our content. Everything we put out performed poorly.

Fair play to Kai in America, he was on the ball and promised they were sorting out how to get the videos back into people's feeds – because it was new to Facebook, their tech teams were still learning. And they did figure it out because after that first few weeks, we were suddenly making money and everything changed. It remains probably the most important moment in our journey with taking LadBaby to the next level. This passion and side project of making videos was suddenly earning us proper money.

It was up and down, and it still is today – you never knew how much you were going to earn. One video could bring in £200 whereas the next one could be twenty grand. It wasn't always based on the number of views, either. It was more about how long people watched it for.

Rox

We'd had the ads for about six months when Facebook approached us about introducing a subscription model.

Mark

Again, it was a trial, just testing the waters to see if there was interest. It would mean people could pay £3.99 a month to sign up and subscribe to our channel and have access to extra content.

Rox

Do you remember the introduction video they wanted us to do, inviting people to subscribe, Mark? It was following the 'best practice' of what creators had done in America.

Mark

Best practice and it was terrible.

Rox

They wanted us to say: 'Hi, everyone. Please support us in our dream of being social media entrepreneurs, together we can make this dream a reality.' More cheese than a Dairylea factory.

Mark

I said to Kai that this sort of thing might work in America with the whole American Dream, positive vibes thing. But it wouldn't work over here.

Rox

Course it wouldn't! Brits are too cynical. People would say: 'I'm not paying for you to sit on your arse at home and make silly videos. Go and get a real job, love!'

And that's why I love the UK.

Mark

We told Kai that we just needed to give people value, entertainment and joy and we were going to try it our way and see if it worked. That meant no hard sell. We wanted to be very honest and upfront with everyone and to make it clear that *nothing* was changing.

So, we did a video saying the only difference was now there was an opportunity to subscribe, but it would be for extra content on top of what we were already putting out. We would still be doing the weekend videos as normal for everyone. That would all stay the same. But for anyone who was interested in seeing some bonus stuff and getting some additional perks, then 'for the price of a pint', they could sign up.

Rox

The extra bits were going out every Monday, Wednesday and Friday and would be a mix of lives, Q&As, playing games, opening fan mail and more videos. We wanted to give people value for the money they'd be paying.

Mark

We still do that today. Mondays, Wednesdays and Fridays – we've stuck to that since 2018. The Turbo zone is something we've done all these years and will keep doing for as long as people enjoy it.

Rox

The Turbo zone is literally the best community of LadBaby fans and followers.

Mark

The numbers aren't anywhere near as high as they were when we first launched, but that's because we stopped advertising it during lockdown. We felt in a cost-of-living crisis when families were struggling, it wasn't appropriate to promote it, but it'll always be part of our online community.

Rox

We often share all our biggest and most exciting news about LadBaby and our family to the group before announcing it to the public.

Mark

In a weird way it's become like our second family. It's a safe space where we can celebrate our biggest moments with the people who care about us the most. We know so many of them by name and it's allowed us to build a bond with them that's closer than anywhere else online.

Rox

But in the beginning it was a gamble. What we'd done was rip up Facebook's rulebook and told them we would do it the way we wanted and how we thought our audience would best respond. We had some brass neck, but we'd also developed a good instinct for what worked and the relationship with our audience was key to that.

Mark

The 'Turbos' was our affectionate nickname for subscribers.

Rox

We were learning on the job, though. And we had no gauge as to what qualified as a success.

Mark

At the end of the first week of subscriptions, we had two thousand people signed up and I remember speaking to Kai and apologising. I thought it was so embarrassing only to have garnered that from the two million we had following.

'Mark,' he said, 'you do know you're now the biggest fan subscription creators in the world?'

Rox

What the actual?

Mark

And it continued to climb to five or six thousand.

Rox

We were the biggest in the world for about two years. There was a lot of interest both from American creators and the Facebook tech team itself in what we were doing to make the subscription model so successful. They flew us over to LA to speak at a Facebook event about how we'd done it. We got picked up from the hotel in a giant SUV with blacked-out windows just like in the movies. Bloody Nora, the security involved just getting us inside, but it was so much fun. Mad but fun.

Mark

When we told the audience we'd compared the monthly fee to the cost of a pint, they all laughed.

Rox

They did! But it wasn't really meant to be funny because that honesty and realness was the heart of our message. Just be yourself, don't lie, be authentic with your audience and never try to put on an act.

People were coming up afterwards like, 'That was amazing, man!' but as far as we were concerned we hadn't done or said anything innovative. We were just doing us, because that is all we knew and all we have ever known.

Mark

And more than two years after starting LadBaby and all those false starts and dashed hopes, thanks to a steadfast refusal to give up, we were making good money for the first time.

Perhaps this was going to work after all . . .

10

When Mum and Dad got the Christmas Number One

Rox

It all started with a chat I had with my mum over a cup of tea. She'd been volunteering at a food bank and she was telling me about how busy they were with families.

'They're just like you and Mark,' she said. 'Mums with young babies . . . the situation out there is desperate.'

I couldn't believe what she was describing. I'd known about the existence of food banks, but had assumed they were used by homeless people who needed a bit of help to get back on their feet. I'd had no idea that there were so many kids going hungry and who were relying on the food banks to get some food in their tummies. Was this really happening in the UK?

I was horrified. I'd thought I was up to date with the news and what was going on – how hadn't I realised there were so many people on the brink? These were people who had jobs and houses and yet they couldn't afford basic essentials.

Mark

This conversation happened at around the same time as we'd been thinking about recording a jokey song about my love of sausage rolls.

The big three things we'd become known for had all come about by accident. My catchphrase 'Yes, mate!' was something I'd said for ever anyway, the success of toolbox video had been a complete surprise and then there were the sausage rolls. I used to go to Greggs a fair bit because it was cheap and cheerful, and people started pointing out in the comments that I seemed to eat an awful lot of sausage rolls.

It wasn't a deliberate thing! I genuinely love sausage rolls. When I was a kid my mum and dad used to make them for Christmas Day. It was a Hoyle tradition.

Rox

Hand on heart, I'd never had a Greggs sausage roll until I met Mark.

Mark
What a deprived childhood.

Rox

He converted me. Obviously I'm now a devoted sausage roll fanatic.

Mark
The more people commented, the more I played up to it, putting sausage rolls into the videos whenever I could. And it was a random tweet that set the cogs turning. Someone wrote that LadBaby should release the song 'We Built This City' but change the 'rock and roll' part of the lyrics to 'sausage rolls'.

I immediately knew we should do it. It would be hilarious if we could rewrite all the lyrics to make them sausage roll-related. We couldn't sing for toffee, but that made it even funnier.

Rox

If you're going to release a novelty song, then Christmas is the time to do it. I'm Bob the Builder's biggest fan, just putting that out there. So that's what we set our sights on, a bit of festive fun.

And all this just so happened to coincide with the talk I'd had with my mum about food banks.

We were doing this silly song, so why not do it in aid of a charity like the Trussell Trust? They ran more than one thousand food banks across the country.

Mark

Suddenly it was happening. Our manager at the time also looked after an indie band who did parody songs on their YouTube channel and he said one of the guys would be up for producing the track. I met him in Costa Coffee in Camden on my lunch break and he was perfect.

Rox

He was such a lovely lad, wasn't he? And so talented. The way he ended up putting the song together with us was genius.

Mark

And then he put us in touch with an indie record label who had some experience in social media songs and they agreed to come on board to release the track. We didn't have a clue what we were doing, but through various contacts, we'd somehow built a team.

We booked two days in a recording studio and the plan was to write the track on the first day and then record it on the second. Alongside our excellent producer, we came up with a perfect homage to the humble sausage roll:

If you've never had one
And don't recognise the taste
It's a cylindrical bit of pork wrapped
In a puff pastry case

Beige, baked and golden
Holier than grace
Grab it whilst it's pipin' hot and
Shove it in your face!

They're party sized to foot long
Listen to your belly groan
Don't you remember
We built this city
We built this city on sausage rolls

Rox

We knew we would need a video to go with the song and the original idea was to do an '(Is This The Way To) Amarillo'-style skit with us walking around various sites in Nottingham. A local ex-BBC producer was recommended to us and he agreed to film it at a very reasonable cost.

Mark

He also suggested doing a bit of filming in the studio as we were recording the song and the footage he got of us behind the scenes turned out to be way better and more fitting than the 'Amarillo' idea. It was a much more natural video and we liked that people would see us as we were.

Rox

The day we came to record it was full on and we only stopped briefly for a Nando's lunch – this would become a tradition, having a Nando's on the day we recorded the Christmas single.

It got to the point where it would have been bad luck if we didn't do it.

Mark

The intention was to get it into the charts and raise some money for the Trussell Trust. One hundred per cent of the profits would go straight to the charity.

Privately between ourselves, we'd nicknamed the track 'number-one song' but it was only ever said in jest. The fact it would go on to beat Mariah and Ariana to bag the top spot and be the 2018 Christmas number one was beyond our wildest dreams.

It always makes me chuckle when I see a pop star celebrating a number-one single or album. A while back I saw Stormzy getting to the top of the charts and he was on Instagram with his team in this swanky office – there were what looked like hundreds of people cheering and partying and cracking open the Cristal.

On the day we found out we'd got the Christmas number one, we were in our living room, just the two of us with a bottle of supermarket Prosecco!

I think the craziest we ever got was after the second single the following year when we ventured to the local Travelodge with some neighbours and had a couple of pints of Fosters.

Rox

And the year after that, I celebrated by falling asleep on the sofa. That's rock 'n' roll for you, kids. We sometimes wondered if we should have upped our game, but that's just how we always did it – we put everything together on a shoestring, no fuss and no fanfare.

Mark

And what's odd about the aftermath of a Christmas number one is how quickly it's all over. Once it's been announced, that's it. Done. The focus shifts as everyone packs up for the holidays and the industry shuts down. We had this utter euphoria, but nowhere to put it and no one to share it with.

Rox

The team said we'd celebrate in the New Year, but that never happened.

Mark

By Boxing Day, literally no one cares! And by the time people come back to work in January, they have absolutely moved on. It's like it never happened at all.

Rox

As soon as January starts, it's all about fitness and 'New Year, New You'. Everyone has forgotten about Christmas and it feels like a lifetime ago.

Mark

We were so naive about how things worked. I thought we'd go into January and still be getting asked questions about it and doing the radio interviews, but it was over. We got used to that in the end, but the first year it was a bit of a shocker.

Rox

The reaction on the street was fabulous, though. I remember going out and about between Christmas and New Year and people would approach us in the street, the park or the supermarket to say congratulations and what an incredible achievement it had been. It was so lovely for people to take the time to come over.

Quite a few came up to say they'd had to use a food bank and thanked us for raising awareness and helping their kids get fed. Hearing those stories was heartbreaking and a striking reminder of the reason we did it in the first place.

Mark
We'd had a Christmas number one; we'd raised money for the Trussell Trust and brought attention to a cause we both cared deeply about. And I think that was the moment we realised we'd achieved something beyond social media. It was the first time something felt so much bigger than us.

Rox
There was also a very strong feeling that if you really put your mind to something, you could do it.

Mark
And if anyone ever breaks into our house, we've now got a readymade weapon. The Official Number One award you get given for getting to the top of the charts is so heavy, it would take out King Kong if it fell on him.

Rox
We keep ours on a shelf but have to lay them flat because we can't risk them falling off and hitting one of the boys. They're lethal!

Mark
We might have had the Christmas number one, but we didn't get invited to the Brit Awards, did we?

Rox
As if. We didn't get invited anywhere!

Mark

Maybe I was wrong, but I thought the Brit Awards was all about celebrating British music. Well, we'd just had a Christmas number one – didn't we qualify for an invite? Apparently not. Despite me DMing the organisers and sponsors, no one ever came back to me and so for a giggle, we bought our own tickets in the nosebleeds for the 2019 awards. We turned up at the O2 wearing matching sausage roll suits, which had been made for us by a follower, and we had a great time outside posing for selfies and filming for our channels.

Rox

Some people could not understand why we weren't even acknowledged and I know a lot of our followers were upset for us. But we were pretty chill about it. We always felt that the music industry as a whole didn't like novelty acts and suspected that we were seen as an embarrassment. And it wasn't as if we wanted to be part of that world anyway.

Mark

Snubbed! But we had our own after-party on the train back to Hemel, with a can of Budweiser and a plastic tumbler of wine.

Rox

Class in a glass. We'd also paid twelve quid for a burger in the O2! A tenner for a wine! And there was nowhere to dance where we were sitting. I decided that from then on, whatever happened, I'd be watching the Brits from the comfort of our sofa in my jarmies.

Mark

Although we *did* go back the following year because we'd received what we thought was an official invite as artists.

Rox

Oh yeah and we were buzzing! We got dressed up in our custom-made sausage roll suits again, ready to walk the red carpet for the night of our lives.

Mark

Only when we got there, we realised that the tickets we'd been allocated weren't for artists or VIPs. We were turned away from the main artist red carpet entrance and instead were ushered into a hotel function room where we had a meal with people who had won their tickets on radio phone-in competitions or blagged them from a mate who did the security for the O2. There was no one from the music industry there and we felt so embarrassed for having thought we'd be sat down in the main arena with all the big-name music-industry people. It was all so cringe, us sitting there sticking out like sore thumbs in those sausage roll suits.

Rox

We were so disappointed. Mark was heartbroken. We did a video about the whole experience and the record label told us that the Brit Awards were less than pleased about it. But we kept the video up.

Mark

We're always grateful and appreciative of being invited to any awards show, but if you've been led to believe you're there in recognition of your achievements and success but you're then sat in the nosebleeds it's a bit of a shock. I think we were naive to think the music industry would show us any respect.

Rox

So that was fun!

Mark

In our house we now call them the Sh*t Awards.

Rox

But, we digress.

Mark

Anyway, with the Christmas number-one dust well and truly settled, we just went back to making videos. It was about LadBaby, parenting and what made us happy, so we found our groove again doing what we did best. One of the videos that got the biggest reaction was when I got Rox Valentine's flowers. Except they were the type of floral arrangement you see in funeral cars and they spelled out the word 'MILF'.

Rox

I just remember accepting those flowers from this poor delivery guy at the door and he didn't know where to look. I couldn't believe it.

Mark

Personalised flowers, Rox. What could be more thoughtful on Valentine's?

Rox

Ha! That brought us back to what we'd been doing before the Christmas number-one madness took over.

Mark

As far as we were concerned, the Christmas single had been a one-off. We'd had a huge amount of fun and raised money for a worthy cause, but it wasn't something we were looking to repeat.

Rox

However . . .

Mark

Towards the end of the summer of 2019, we had a phone call from the Trussell Trust, who told us how far the money raised had gone and the difference it had made to the food banks. But there were now more than fourteen million people in the UK living below the poverty line – over four million of these were children. And that number was only going to rise.

Rox

The charity had benefited not just from the money raised but also the publicity – they'd never had so much press interest and that amount of exposure was invaluable. It had given them a platform and there had been a big increase in donations from people who hadn't been aware of the charity prior to our Christmas single.

They asked if we would help again with another song.

Mark

I wasn't sure if we could do it, but at the same time there were a lot of our audience also asking us to go again. They said their kids were still playing our version of 'We Built This City' and it was doing their heads in so could we please write another one to replace it!

Rox

And who were we to deny the people what they wanted?

Mark

After discussing it with Rox, we came to the conclusion: why the hell not?

Rox

We couldn't promise to replicate the success of the previous year, but whatever we did would raise some money and go towards helping people who really needed it this Christmas.

Mark
Oh lordy, here we go again . . .

11

The Beatles, Amy Winehouse ... LadBaby?

Mark

Not everyone was quite as eager for us to go for another Christmas number one. Our manager told us no way should we even consider it.

'You're only going to embarrass yourselves,' he said. 'What you did was a fluke, you won't be able to repeat it. Don't do it.'

Rox

We felt like he was concerned we would ruin our credibility.

Mark

Er, what credibility? It was a sausage roll song and it was for charity. Credibility wasn't a factor here.

Rox

We considered whether he might be right and to'd and fro'd on it for a while. But we felt like it was the right thing for us to do.

Mark

I arranged a face-to-face meeting to tell him that I didn't think we were aligned any more. We had different visions for LadBaby and it was probably best that we parted ways.

Rox

It was the right thing to do, but it left us out on our own. It's actually very hard to find good social media management. It's not like being a TV talent or a music artist. Social media is, by its nature, a constantly evolving industry and there aren't many management teams who understand it. It's still so new and everyone's feeling as they go.

Mark

Through a contact at LADbible, we found new representation and they were instantly on board with supporting a second song. We asked our followers on Instagram which track we should do next and there was an almost unanimous victory for *I Love Rock 'n' Roll* which (obviously) we would change to *Sausage Rolls*.

The record label was up for it, our cameraman was ready and available. We were getting the band back together!

Rox

But then we heard that the producer who had been such an important part of the first song's success didn't want to do it. It was a straight no from him. He was moving away from parody songs and wanted to be taken seriously as a producer.

I was so upset.

Mark

We didn't feel like we could do it without him.

Rox

But at the same time, we'd already given our word to the Trussell Trust and we couldn't let them down.

Mark

By now it was the first week of November and the clock was ticking. The record label suggested another producer we might like to meet as an alternative.

This guy had his own studio at home, which we thought sounded cool. If someone has a home studio, they know their stuff, right? When we went round to his place in north London, I think we were expecting Dr Dre to answer the door.

Rox

Instead, there was a bloke wearing a dressing gown and sliders with white socks, eating a bowl of Cornflakes.

Mark

I said: 'Oh hello, are we in the right place?'

'Yeah, yeah. Come in.'

'You're the guy with the studio?'

'Yep, we'll do it in the garage.'

'Er, OK. Cool.'

Rox

It was all very bougie, wasn't it? We even had a cup of tea with his wife and kids as they got ready for the school run.

Mark

He didn't get changed. He spent all day in his dressing gown and sliders but fair dos, he was great at what he did! We rewrote the lyrics with him and although it wasn't the song we'd intended to write – there was much more innuendo – it worked.

Rox would kick it off with the immortal lines:

> I saw him standing there in the bakery
> Holding the biggest sausage roll I've ever seen
> Didn't know it would turn me on
> But I'd never seen one so long
> And I knew it was gonna be wrong
> But I want meat, yeah, meat
> Baked in puff pastry
> Yeah, I want meat, yeah, meat

Rox

Cough, cough. It was a bit saucy, wasn't it?

Mark

We were desperate to record it at London's famous Abbey Road Studios. That was the big dream because we wanted to bill the whole thing as a massive upgrade from the year before. The label tried to get us a space there but were told they were completely booked out for the whole of November and December. We were gutted.

Rox

We asked them to keep us updated in case somebody cancelled and then started to scout around for a plan B.

Mark

And then they rang back a few days later and said they had just converted an old storeroom into a tiny studio ... might that work?

'Is it definitely in Abbey Road?' I asked.

'Well yeah. It used to be a cupboard but it's definitely Abbey Road.'

'Brilliant, we'll take it.'

The Beatles, Kate Bush, Radiohead and Amy Winehouse had all recorded in that building. Now LadBaby would be added to the list, albeit from the store cupboard.

Rox

The idea for the video was that we were breaking into Abbey Road, disguised as workmen, to record the single. Obviously, we recreated the iconic zebra crossing shot made famous by The Beatles.

Mark

At the end of the video, we'd be fake-arrested by a police officer, frogmarched out of the building in handcuffs and thrown in the back of a police van. I'm good friends with someone who works for the police in real life and she got permission from her force to take part in her uniform and bring along a vehicle.

Rox

We wore our sausage roll tracksuits for the whole day.

Mark

Always on brand!

Rox

And our new producer was there. He'd got dressed by then, thank goodness.

Mark

People said follow-up novelty songs always flop. Look at Mr Blobby. Did you know he released another single two years after his 1993 Christmas number one? Of course you didn't! 'Christmas in Blobbyland' reached the dizzy heights of thirty-six and then sank without trace. The joke was only funny the first time and that's what everyone said would happen to us.

But with poverty rates in the UK worse than they had been a year ago, it felt more important than ever. And it was the song our followers had asked for so there were people lined up and ready to buy it. We were quietly confident we could at least cause a bit of a stir.

Rox

All I knew was that I didn't want it to fail for the charity. That was the drive and the main thing on all our minds. As long as it raised money, it would be a win.

Mark

But we were fighting what felt like a losing battle with the traditional media. The press weren't interested this time around and neither was TV. Radio stations never played us. The record label PR told us that unless we were number one or two at the midweek point, no one would care. So we did the campaigning for downloads via our channels and our followers loved it.

Rox

And when we got to midweek, we were in the lead at number one, which is when it all kicked off again.

Mark

Suddenly everybody wanted to speak to us and we really needed to be based in London for the next couple of days. We thought it would be funny to stay at the ultimate rock 'n' roll quarters – the Hard Rock Hotel.

Rox

We were doing as much media as we possibly could because with one day to go, the song at number two, 'Own It', which was a Stormzy, Ed Sheeran and Burna Boy collab, wasn't far behind us in numbers. We'd seen off Ariana Grande in 2018, but imagine going up against Ed Sheeran and Stormzy, two of the best musicians Britain has ever produced!

And I loved their song. In any other week of the year, I'd have been happy for it to get to number one.

Mark

I banned her from listening to it.

Rox

I had to wait a week to download or even stream it because we didn't want to do anything to tip the balance in their favour!

Mark

The day of the countdown arrived, 20 December 2019. We did the whole thing with Scott Mills again, recording a reaction for if we'd done it and another for if we hadn't. And then we went back to the Hard Rock Hotel and turned on Radio 1.

Rox

We went live with our fans and followers and waited, even more nervously than the previous year. Wham!, Dua Lipa, Lewis Capaldi were at five, four and three. As predicted, it was between us and Stormzy and Ed.

Mark

And when Scott announced us as the 2019 Christmas number one, I broke down.

Rox

I screamed so loudly, someone came up to the room to check everything was all right, thinking we were having a domestic. That second number one floored me. I hadn't dared to believe that it might be possible.

Mark

It was pure disbelief. To have done it once was incredible. To do it again was inconceivable.

Rox

Our phones started going mad and we gave some interviews while still physically shaking.

Mark

Then we celebrated over a few drinks in the hotel with Rox's mum and sister, and I was so hungover the next day that I was green while filming a news interview with the BBC.

Rox

Although this crazy thing had happened, we still had our normal life to get back to. We were only a couple of days away from Christmas, Santa was coming and I had to pick up the turkey and remember to buy the cranberry sauce.

That's kind of what our life is like. It goes, 'WHOA! THIS IS COMPLETELY BANANAS!' And then back to reality again.

Mark

There was something else rather lovely and unexpected to come out of that number one. The original 'I Love Rock 'n' Roll' was written back in the seventies by an American guy called Alan Merrill, with a writing credit to Jake Hooker. Alan, god love him, reached out to us afterwards to say he'd never had a UK number one before and he thanked us for finally giving him that honour.

Rox

Very sadly, he died a few months later during the pandemic due to complications brought on by Covid. His daughter wrote to us saying she wanted to let us know that we'd made him so happy, getting that song to number one. What a legend.

Mark

Throughout all this, I'd still been working my nine to five as a graphic designer. About halfway through 2019, I'd dropped to a four-day week, but even that was feeling increasingly unmanageable as LadBaby continued to grow.

Just before Christmas, I'd been to see my boss and explained how difficult I was finding it to straddle both careers. I'd wanted to be a graphic designer since I was a kid and I'd worked extremely hard to make it happen. I loved my job and didn't want to quit, but the only way I was going to be able to continue was by going down to three days a week.

My boss told me no. It was LadBaby or the job and I had to make a choice.

Backed into a corner, I chose LadBaby.

Rox

It wasn't a responsible decision. Social media wasn't a stable, established career option. The income varied from one video to the next and we didn't know what the short-term future was, let alone the longer term.

Mark

Everyone around me thought I was mad to quit my job, and my parents especially didn't understand the decision. As far as they could see, I'd been to uni and had a career in graphic design with a company pension and now I was giving it all up to make joke videos. They asked what would happen if it all stopped tomorrow? Which was fair enough.

But we'd had a steady stream of income from Facebook for some time now. I was making more in a month than my annual salary and so it felt 'safe' in that sense. We had an accountant who was making sure our taxes were sorted and above board.

He actually became a life coach as well as an accountant because I would ask him for reassurance that it was going to be OK. True to form, and just like my parents, I was thinking of the 'what ifs' and he was there to talk me down again and tell me we had more than enough money coming in for it to be absolutely fine.

Rox

We were both aware that this could grind to a halt at any point, but we've always been quite careful with our earnings. We're not the sort of people to go out and buy fast cars or designer clothes and handbags. I still shop in B&M, Poundland and Aldi. I remember the feeling of having nothing and I want to protect our future and what we've built.

Mark

We were earning more than we'd ever imagined, but we only took what we needed to pay our mortgage and bills, and told our accountant to save the rest.

Rox

I totally understand why our parents were sceptical and worried, but this was something we had to do. It was an opportunity to give it a really good go.

However, none of us ever know what's around the corner. And, proving that point, just a couple of months after Mark quit his job, Covid struck.

The world locked down and the future had never felt more uncertain.

Mark

We were as terrified and dismayed by what was happening as anyone else. We were frightened for the health of our families and the impact on the wider world. We missed our loved ones terribly and hated not knowing when we'd get to hold them again.

We were also hyper aware that lockdown could be about to place us in choppy financial waters. I'd just given up my day job and so we were self-employed in a precarious industry and every brand we'd been working with pulled out.

Rox

With the exception of our partnership with Walkers, everything stopped overnight.

Mark

That was scary. But at the same time, there was an instant explosion in the numbers of views our videos were getting, and the revenue generated from that plugged the gap left by the brands. Before Covid, our audience had started levelling out. We had a great community, but it hadn't been growing at the same rate of knots as it had in the past.

Rox

Lockdown spiked the hell out of our channels. It went mad as people were seeking out humour and fun – anything to help them get through the day. It was such a tough time for everyone and we thought the best thing would be to carry on doing our normal silly stuff.

Mark

We were constantly thinking of ways we could try and make people smile, and it usually boiled down to us being daft. A lot of people say to me even now that we helped them through lockdown just by making them laugh.

Rox

So many of the people we talk to now found us during lockdown.

Mark

Our only plan was to make content that would give people a bit of a lift. People were stuck at home, often with young children, and so we came up with loads of ideas around how to keep your kids entertained during lockdown.

We filmed a video featuring thirty games that could all be done using rolls of tape. At Easter, we bought Kinder Eggs, put them in a Nerf gun and fired them over the fence to our neighbours, who were isolating.

Rox

We bought a pair of those mini greenhouses with the plastic covers and me and my friend from down the road each sat in one, two metres apart, and drank wine.

'When Mum hacks wine time with best friend' is what we called that one.

Mark

That was hilarious. The two of you sat out in the street in your greenhouses is an image I'll never forget.

I recreated Legoland in our back garden because we'd planned to go there for Kobe's second birthday in May and now that couldn't happen. I used giant fake Lego bricks, which were cheap on Amazon, set up various Lego stations and nailed colourful paper all the way round the fence so everything looked vibrant.

We took the boys to Legoland for real a little while ago and they both said my home version was better! And way cheaper.

Rox

Do you remember the response to the McDonald's drive-thru hack?

Mark

Ahh, everyone loved that one. Phoenix had just turned four and he'd asked for a Happy Meal for his birthday tea. But obviously all the McDonald's were shut.

I took my permitted daily hour of exercise to head down to the nearest drive-thru and, even though it was closed, I walked round the site and filmed my point of view from ordering at the intercom ('Hello, welcome to McDonald's. Please can I take your order?') to picking the meal up at the hatch.

When I got home, I superimposed footage of me, dressed in the grey of the McDonald's uniform, on to the kiosk window where the orders are collected as if I was the customer assistant. It was like a drive-thru simulator.

Rox

Mark used tape to put road tracks on the living room floor and then Phoenix got into his Little Tikes Cozy Coupe while we played the two-minute film on the TV as he drove along. And when it got to the end, Mark handed him a Happy Meal-style box in person, containing a toy and some fries and nuggets, which we'd made at home.

Mark

Then I uploaded the simulator on its own to YouTube so other parents could recreate the McDonald's drive-thru experience and it went absolutely crazy.

Rox

So many people were commenting and getting in touch to say they'd played it and how much the kids had loved it.

Mark

We had quite a few messages from families with children with additional needs who had especially enjoyed it and that was just fantastic to hear.

Rox

Of course, Covid and lockdown had massive ramifications for people's mental health and finances. The food banks continued to operate, but also had to adapt and try to deliver parcels directly to people who weren't able to leave their homes. Over one million food parcels were handed out in the first six months of the pandemic.

Mark

We were in regular contact with the Trussell Trust throughout and they were seriously worried about whether they'd be able to keep all their food banks open.

Rox

Their donated goods had plummeted because people weren't physically going to the supermarkets where they would normally drop extra items at the collection points.

Mark

As with the second single, we had never planned to do a third. We truly hadn't. But the spiralling circumstances meant the charity was needed more than ever and we started to think about how we might possibly do it. Especially since we were all still living under restrictions that would make getting together to record in a studio tricky, to say the least.

Rox

Me and Mark aren't rule breakers – we always do as we're told! So we were working out the logistics of putting something together, including a video, while complying with the two-metre distance rule and face masks and all that malarkey.

Mark

We contacted our usual cameraman and he said yes. The record label agreed to go again as well. But we decided to see if there was another producer available.

Rox

I couldn't take 'dressing-gown gate' again.

Mark

We were put in touch with a guy called Jamie who would end up doing the next three songs with us. This time, we'd chosen to parody 'Don't Stop Believin'' by Journey, which we changed to 'Don't Stop Me Eatin'', and we had enough confidence to write all the lyrics ourselves. We were chart veterans by this time!

Rox

I think there was also an element of, 'OK, we're never going to get a third number one so let's throw caution to the wind.'

Mark

We knew we wanted to release two versions of the single because together they would count towards one chart placement. As well as the track the two of us would record, we needed to get a big name – a real musician – involved for the second. Someone who would surprise people and take the whole project up a few notches.

The TV booker at the record label said she used to work with Boyzone and would see if she could get Ronan Keating.

'That would be amazing,' I said. 'Would he be willing to sing the most ridiculous song?'

'We can only ask the question,' she replied.

She set up a Zoom meeting with me and Ronan.

Rox

You can only *imagine* what I went through that day, as a nineties boy band superfan.

Mark

Ronan said he'd seen what we did at Christmas and was keen to help.

He asked, 'What would you like me to do?'

'Just turn up and sing this song about sausage rolls as straight as you can, as if it's a love song. Ignore what the lyrics are saying and just belt it out earnestly and deadly serious.'

'OK,' he said. 'Let's try it.'

12

Third Time Lucky

Mark

I want it to be known that Ronan Keating is a living legend. He came down to the studio that day and he absolutely smashed it.

Rox

Genuinely. What a top bloke. He was *so* good and so encouraging to me, too, knowing I was feeling the pressure to perform this duet with him.

'Come on, Roxy,' he'd say. 'Let's go, Roxy!'

Every so often I'd look over and see Ronan Keating singing the lyrics we'd written and think, 'What is my life?!'

Mark

With the lyrics, we'd wanted to see if we could turn this song into something that actually touched people's hearts while still getting the sausage roll references in. No mean feat.

We'd filmed people volunteering at a food bank and would use this footage in the video to the beautiful strains of Ronan Keating in full flow. Could this silly song make people *feel* something?

Just a sausage roll
On a year that's outta control
Feeding the nation is our Christmas goal
Just a pastry treat
And when my family finally meet
We'll share a foot-long through a plastic sheet

Rox

It was a risk for Ronan. He was presenting on *The One Show* and he had a career as a solo artist to think about. Me and Mark are always told that we're not really 'desirable' or 'aspirational'. We're a family who are seen as a bit of a joke and for him to set all that aside and do this for the charity was very noble of him. I'll always have a lot of respect for that man.

Mark

He was like Rox's hype man in the studio.

Rox

There was a big note at the finish that I couldn't get. It was the big climax to the song and it terrified me!

'Roxy, you've got to hit the note!'

'It's too much, Ronan. I'm not a singer. I can't do it.'

'Just go for it, Roxy!'

I honestly don't even know what happened, but I gave it all my welly and somehow this powerhouse of a note came out of my mouth. And it kept on coming! The people in the sound booth were jumping up and down, Ronan was standing there open-mouthed and my head had just gone.

We all collapsed laughing with shock. You can hear the laughter on the track, with Ronan giving it, 'Go on, Roxy!'

Mark

The reason I'm not in that video is because I spent the whole time p***ing myself, which would have taken away from the sensitive feel we were going for.

Rox

There's one shot on the video where you can see Mark laughing his absolute tits off at the sight and sound of me and Ronan Keating singing about sausage rolls.

Mark

Ronan kindly pulled a few strings and got us on *The One Show* sofa in the run-up to the Christmas countdown.

Rox

We owe him a great debt of gratitude for everything he did. And he only ever asked for a sausage roll in return!

Mark

The Top 40 that year was being announced on Christmas Day itself, by which time we were all living under lockdown restrictions again due to the second Covid wave.

    We knew it was looking good for another number one. Pre-orders alone were about sixty thousand, which was around the same as the entire sales of the second single.

Rox

Those numbers were insane, but we tried not to get distracted by them. We were slightly worried by the news that Ed Sheeran had suddenly decided to release his single 'Afterglow' on 21 December, just four days before the countdown – if there was a last-minute stampede for that, then it could scupper our chances.

Mark

On Christmas Day, we went live from our garden shed, tuned in as usual to Scott Mills and the Official Chart on Radio 1. We'd known that we'd been way out in front on the pre-orders, but we'd asked the label not to update us any further on that.

Rox

We wanted to find out at the same time as our followers, who were all joining us, having eaten their Christmas dinners.

Mark

It was such a special moment when it was announced that we'd done it. We'd beaten Jess Glynne, Mariah and Wham! to the number one. Ed Sheeran's late surge hadn't managed to put a dent in our chances and we were now on a par with the Spice Girls, who'd had three back-to-back Christmas number ones in the nineties. And to do that on Christmas Day felt even more beautiful. Three in a row.

Rox

People were sending us videos of their kids jumping around and screaming, celebrating this third number one. To see the joy was wonderful and, of course, it had raised another big chunk of money for the Trussell Trust, not to mention the huge levels of press and exposure it brought them in probably their hardest year.

Mark

We were delighted for Ronan as well. He'd never had a Christmas number one before and we bought an extra Official Number One award for him as a thank you for everything he'd done.

Rox

That was such a crazy Christmas. We'd also launched a special sausage roll-flavoured crisp range from Walkers. The advert had been filmed back in August on a street in Watford and they'd made it look really Christmassy with carol singers, fairy lights and fake snow.

Mark

I don't think I've ever seen Rox so happy.

Rox

I was nearly crying because I was so delighted with life. It was Christmas in August and I was dressed as an elf! It doesn't get much better than that. There were so many big names in that ad, including Mr Walkers himself, Gary Lineker.

Mark

They also had me and Tony Mortimer from East 17 arguing about how many Christmas number ones we'd both had. They'd dressed him in a white puffa coat with the fluffy fur trim, just like the 'Stay' video from 1994.

Rox

I've got that very coat now! Tony gave it to me at the end and I asked him to sign it. He gave me his shoes, and all. So I've got the Tony Mortimer 'Stay' coat and shoes in my house and they are my prized possessions.

Mark

Whenever we were involved in conversations with brands who could make a difference, we would use that access to secure help for the food banks. So we'd asked Walkers to help out the Trussell Trust and they agreed to donate 5p from every packet sold.

Rox

We'd also made it very clear with Walkers that we wouldn't share anything commercial after 1 December. That was the cut-off point and we ring-fenced the run-up to Christmas to promote only the Trussell Trust and the new single. For us, it didn't feel appropriate for that to be an advertising period and so we also turned off all the ads from YouTube and Facebook like we'd done every year so none of our content was monetised during that time.

We wanted all the focus on the charity, not on me and Mark. That was the only thing that felt right.

Mark

Although things were going well professionally, there were some issues behind the scenes that were causing a bit of distress.

Someone had taken it upon themselves to mark the location of our home on Google Maps – if you opened the app and typed in 'LadBaby' it dropped a big red pin right at our front door. The first we knew of it was when we noticed a steady stream of inquisitive visitors to the street.

Rox

Our kitchen was at the front and I'd often be washing up by the window when I'd spot people walking back and forth trying to peer in. Or they'd drive past really slowly. It started to feel quite scary, especially if I was on my own in the house with the kids.

Mark

Early one morning there was a knock at the door. When I looked through the peephole, there was no one there but a motorbike had been left on the doorstep and a handwritten letter had been pushed through the letterbox.

'Hi Mark and Rox,' it read. 'I know somebody who told me you lived in this area and I found your address. I would love you to help promote my motorbike business. I'm leaving this bike here and will come back and collect it in seven days. Please can you make me two videos on your Instagram and Facebook and tag my account? Thanks.'

Rox

Er, what? We were in complete shock, we didn't know anything about this person or business. We could see a van we didn't recognise parked at the end of the road and put two and two together, guessing that the guy was in it, waiting to see us come out and collect the bike.

Mark

I said to Rox if we just don't leave the house, eventually he'll think he might have the wrong address. He won't want to leave his motorbike there, so we just have to wait until he gives up and goes.

Rox

We stayed in the house for the whole day; it was a case of who would crack first!

Mark

And when it started to get dusky, sure enough he got out of the van, picked up the bike and off he went.

Rox

We can laugh at that now, but at the time I hated people knowing where we lived.

Mark

It was an intrusion and pretty unnerving, but we didn't know what to do and felt powerless to stop it. There had been a much scarier incident one night during the first 2020 lockdown. I answered a door knock at about 9 p.m. and there was a bloke standing and pointing something straight in my face. It turned out to be a phone, but for a split second I feared the worst and thought it was a knife.

'It *is* you!' he said. 'I found you on Google Maps. Can I have a photo?'

Conscious that Rox was upstairs with the boys and not wanting to antagonise anything, I agreed to the picture.

'Where's Rox and the kids?' he asked. 'I need to get a photo with them as well.'

'No, mate. They're in bed.'

'Go and wake them up then.'

'I'm not going to wake them all mate, I'm sorry.'

'Oh, I'll come back tomorrow, then.'

This was overstepping the line and I had to say something.

'Mate,' I said, 'I'm not being funny, but this is our home. If I see you in town, I'd be more than happy for you to get a photo with all of us. But I'd really appreciate it if you didn't come back to the house.'

And that's when he turned.

'Oh yeah? You're not f***ing like this online, are you? I'll come back whenever I want and I'll tell everyone else where you f***ing live as well.'

He got in his car and zoomed off. I was left quite shaken.

Rox

I was too, when Mark told me what had happened. I suddenly didn't feel safe in my own home.

Mark

We phoned the police, not to report it as such, but just to log it in case he did come back. It had frightened me and I wanted some sort of record of it. They sent a couple of officers down to see us the next day.

'How did he know you?' asked one of them.

'He doesn't know us; he just watches our videos.'

'What videos?'

'On social media. We make videos for our online audience, that's our job. He's obviously found out where we live.'

'Right,' said the officer, closing her notebook. 'I think the best thing you can do is stop doing these videos.'

Rox

I was like, 'What?'

'I mean, it's kind of your own fault,' she said. 'You're compromising your own safety and you shouldn't be putting your family on there. Apart from that advice, there's not much we can do.'

Mark

I was gobsmacked that this was all they had to say. I told her this was what I did for a living, this was how I put food on the table.

I admit that I probably hadn't been as cautious as I could or should have been when we first started doing this. I used to film the front of our house and out on the street and it would have been easily identifiable to anyone who knew the area or who wanted to track us down.

Rox

But right at the beginning, we only had friends and family followers. We didn't think it would become so big and the need to protect our privacy wasn't something we'd considered back then.

Mark

I asked the officer if she could give us any more advice and she said to get a Ring doorbell. That was it.

Rox

I tortured myself over how differently the situation with the bloke at the door could have gone. I kept thinking of the boys and whether they were safe living here. As parents, that's our most important job, isn't it? Keeping our children safe.

The attention on us felt intense and it became more apparent post-lockdown. Sometimes we'd get stopped on the street and people would ask for a cuddle with Kobe or try and chat to Nix, which felt too much – although we've still never turned down a photo with anyone.

Mark

I wanted to work out how our address had ended up on Google Maps and after a bit of investigating, I realised that when we'd set up our limited company, I'd registered it at our house. I hadn't given it a second thought or twigged that anyone could go on to Companies House, look up LadBaby and have all this information right in front of them.

And that's when we started to think seriously about the possibility of moving somewhere we'd be less exposed.

Rox

We didn't need to be based anywhere in particular to do our jobs, so we had a lot of freedom when deciding where to go. My dad was in Kent and my mum was in London, while Mark's family were in Nottingham, and it made sense to move closer to one or other side of the family.

Mark

In Nottingham, where property prices were cheaper than the south-east, we could get a bigger house and Rox had visited enough over the years to be familiar with the city. So we started looking there.

Rox

House-hunting during a pandemic wasn't easy, but when we went to see the house we eventually ended up buying, I had a good feeling about it as soon as I stepped through the front door. It felt safe. It was such a lovely space and the garden wasn't overlooked so it was all very private and I could see us being happy there.

Mark

Since moving there in February 2021, we've done things differently in terms of what we show of the house. We saw it as a chance to start afresh and we've never filmed the front of it and we only shoot in certain rooms.

Rox

And never in the boys' bedrooms. That is their private space and I will always protect it. I wanted our family home to feel like a safe haven again, so we've been super careful to give the boys the privacy all kids deserve growing up.

Mark

We couldn't get used to the size of this new place, though. For the first few months we only lived in about a quarter of it. It was a far bigger house than either of us had ever lived in before. Being honest, I was also petrified about how our followers would perceive the move.

Rox

The success of LadBaby meant we'd been able to afford to buy this bigger place and I felt so lucky to own the sort of home I could only have dreamed of when I was growing up. But this new house didn't look like other people's houses and Mark was worried people would judge us for it, or see us differently to the family they knew. Our circumstances might have changed, but we hadn't, not one bit. We had to hope our followers realised that and stuck with us.

Mark

For me, those worries overshadowed all the joy and excitement of moving. We'd been in that same house in Hemel for the whole of LadBaby; that's where we'd built our channel and our relationship with the fans. That was where people knew us.

Rox

We thought everyone would hate us, didn't we?

Mark

So much of our content in the beginning had been based around money-saving hacks and tips. Would the house move jar with what we fundamentally stood for? Would people not like us because they thought we'd 'changed'?

Rox

Although we were comfortable now, we knew what it was like to struggle for money. The incident in Aldi, where I hadn't had the 70p to pay for my shopping, had only been four years before.

Mark

Nearly a year into the pandemic, the country was now in a second, even more financially backbreaking lockdown. People were going through hell. The last thing they wanted to see was us moving to a bigger house. I didn't want to upset anyone or make them feel bad about their situation.

Rox

We're not showy people. I don't believe in flaunting wealth when everyone is just doing what they've got to do to get through life. So we didn't make a big deal of moving house. We just did it quietly and didn't turn it into something we 'announced'.

Mark

House moves and house tours are so popular on YouTube and every YouTuber does them. And I guess we could have made a successful video encompassing all of that. But it didn't feel right. Apart from a brief mention on Instagram stories that we were moving house that day, we didn't acknowledge it.

Rox

And we never have since.

Mark

With hindsight I think *we* wrestled with the thought of us changing far more than our audience did. Our followers have always supported us no matter what and have been well happy for us whatever has come our way. It was probably our struggle more than theirs. I'd always heard people talk about imposter syndrome and never really understood it, but now I did.

Rox

When you grow up working class, you don't forget the hardships and where you came from. That's what defines you and makes you who you are. There are a lot of joyous things that we've struggled to celebrate over the years.

Mark

I've never really regarded our number ones as 'ours'. I wouldn't dream of claiming they belonged to LadBaby.

Rox

We are so proud to have been a part of it but we see them as belonging to the Trussell Trust and to the general public who all bought and streamed the songs – we just helped out with the silly bit in the middle.

Mark

In many ways I feel guilty for our success. I've always felt like we didn't deserve it. That's the truth and I don't know why or where that comes from, but I can't help it. It's maybe because of how things were at school when I was made to feel like I wasn't good enough. And to be completely honest I also had a number of people around me who I felt weren't happy for us.

Rox

Mark had that way more than me when we moved. Everyone in my life was proud of me and celebrated the growth, but that wasn't true for Mark.

Mark

I think a bit of envy swept through some of the people around me. They wanted to be happy for me but struggled with the fact it had happened to me and not them.

Rox

Which I totally get. Our life had changed quite a lot in a short space of time.

Mark

I don't know, but I think that imposter syndrome is always going to be there for me. But the thought of coming across as braggy makes my stomach turn.

Rox

Slap bang in the middle of the house move came what was easily my biggest career moment yet. Over my years on this planet, I've been a gloriously vast array of dress sizes. I've been a size twelve and a size twenty-two and everything in between and I've been happy regardless.

I feel strongly that no matter what size you are, you should be able to dress however you want. No one should have to hide away.

I'm a curvy girl and have always loved clothes and using style and colour to express myself. I'd be asked several times a day by followers where my dress was from or my top or where I liked to shop. So when the online fashion brand In The Style approached me about doing a collection, I jumped at the chance.

After picking myself up off the floor, that is.

Mark

This would be the first time Rox had done something through LadBaby that didn't involve me or the kids.

Rox

This was huge for me. The timing was *wild*, what with the big move, but crikey, it would be worth it. And the first collection would be pyjamas, which are literally my favourite item of clothing.

From the start I said the range would have to go up to a size twenty-eight because I wanted to create for everyone. I was so excited. Before having my babies, I'd been a business girl in ad land and, in some ways, it felt like that dream of a career had gone.

Now I was going back to work and I could feel my creative juices starting to flow.

Mark

It was full on for Rox, but she was determined to be completely hands on with every aspect of the collection. I could see how rewarding she was finding it.

Rox

Fabrics, patterns, design – I was across the whole process and I was overjoyed to be creating again, but this time only for women. My main aim was to make fashion fun for everybody and every *body*. Sod the beige, black and grey pieces that girls of a certain size are forced to wear through lack of choice. Let's do rainbow pyjamas that scream happiness!

It was coming out on Mother's Day 2021, so we added slogans such as 'Just another manic mum day' to the tops. And I pushed hard to make every set as affordable as possible – we managed to keep everything around the twenty quid mark.

Mark

I'll never forget when it went live for the first time – things were selling out within minutes.

Rox

I never expected it to go like that and then to get such wonderful feedback from the women who had bought my PJs was indescribable. I received messages saying, 'Thank you for doing this in my size – I've not felt so comfortable in such a long time.'

We went on to do quarterly collections, expanding into dresses, jumpsuits and swimwear. It was carnage in the best possible way.

Mark

We were driving back from Morrisons one day when Roxanne started shrieking. She'd spotted a woman walking down the road wearing a jumpsuit from her collection.

Rox

I spotted my clothes on other people instantly. I knew the fabrics, the style of the shoulders, the nipped-in waists, the pockets and the crazy prints. I'd bump into women wearing my dresses on nights out and they'd say, 'Thank you for making a dress that my boobs fit into!'

Mark

Quite often I'd have women walk up to me and say, 'Look!'

And then they'd gesture to the dress they were wearing. 'It's one of Rox's.'

Obviously I didn't have a clue, but I'd say thank you, that they looked lovely and that I'd pass it on to the missus.

Rox

I used to get a lot of husbands or partners approaching me.

'She won't come and say herself,' they'd say, 'but she's not felt the same about herself since having a baby and I just want to thank you for making her feel confident again.'

That gave me life. Because I knew how having a baby changes your body and how easy it is to lose a bit of your identity in the aftermath.

Helping women feel good about themselves boosted my own confidence and made me more assertive with my decision-making.

Mark

After a year, In The Style partnered with George, and Rox's collections ended up going into Asda and selling to the mass market.

Rox

That is one of the best feelings I've ever had. I was one of three In The Style collaborators who were selected to launch into Asda. On the first day of sales, Mark filmed me walking into our local store and if you find that video, you'll see that I could not cope with what was happening. Seeing my clothes – The LadBaby Mum range – with their own section in Asda was beyond comprehension.

Mark

I got emotional, too. And we both just about fainted when we saw a woman have a look at one of the jumpers, check it over and then put it in her trolley.

Rox

What. A. Moment. Silly, really.

Mark

No, not silly at all. I was bursting with pride for you. And you should never lose the buzz for moments like that.

Rox

I won't. I really won't.

I did about ten collections for In The Style over two years, including a special every now and again like when the World Cup was on. But we ran into various issues with freight, which meant supply couldn't keep up with the demand. People would go into Asda and everything they wanted would be sold out or unavailable.

Mark

Global shipping had become an absolute nightmare and meant the prices skyrocketed.

Rox

People were messaging me saying they couldn't get hold of any of my clothes. But it was totally out of our control.

Mark

Rox would launch the latest collection online but there simply wasn't enough stock to put it into Asda as well. And so everything dwindled down because they couldn't supply it.

Rox

I did a swim collection and it wasn't anything like what it could have been. It had the potential to be incredible for the plus-size market and I had very high standards for curvy women, but the pricing wasn't right, it wasn't made with the fabric I'd requested and the stock levels were all over the place.

It reached a point where I felt this wasn't me any more. In the past I'd been able to take on board feedback from my customers and go to the team with tweaks – adding an extra button for women with big busts here or putting extra length into the bum section of the jumpsuits there – and it would get done.

Mark

It wasn't going to be possible to have as much say in how the clothes were made.

Rox

I didn't want to create clothes that didn't fit with my standards and which didn't reflect my values. I also didn't feel like I had the right team around me to create what had been selling so well at the beginning. And then they took the pyjama range away because they couldn't get the fabrics that I loved. PJs were my top sellers, so I was gutted.

They wanted me to do another year and offered me a six-figure deal to stay on, but because of my concerns, the fabrics had changed, the costs had gone up, I wouldn't have been able to do what I wanted to and I'd have to relinquish a fair bit of creative freedom. I said no.

Mark

It was such a lot of money to turn down. But if Rox wasn't happy and didn't feel she could deliver the products her audience wanted, then she couldn't sign the contract. I told her I'd stand with her and support her on whatever decision she made.

Rox

I had to walk away from it and it was extremely upsetting. I felt like I'd failed. I spent the next six months in a state of grief, not really knowing what to do with myself.

Even now, people ask when my next collection is coming and it breaks my heart, because I can't do it on my own. It makes me so sad that I don't have that in my life any more.

Mark

Rox had this feeling that she'd let people down. So many women had adored her collections and had found clothes they loved for the first time in years.

Rox

It was such a shame because the mum market is very over-looked in fashion. I'm not a trendy twenty-year-old, but I like to look and feel good while wearing clothes that are practical for the day-to-day trials and tribulations of mumming. We don't want to wear crop tops or short skirts. We want active-wear but to go about our daily business in, rather than to run on the bloody treadmill.

I'd love to have the chance to create again, but it has to be with the right team. I'll never be someone who just puts my name to something that I don't feel represents me or the millions of real women who follow me.

Mark

We've had approaches from fashion brands, but never one that would allow Rox to get involved and do what she's good at.

Rox

I've had meetings with various brands, but it's only ever with a view to me promoting an existing range rather than creating it myself. I might be wrong, but I just feel there's so much untapped potential and that's where I want to be.

Maybe it'll happen again but, in the meantime, I'll just do me. Dopamine dressing, that's what I love. I'm grateful to have had the opportunity and I'll be proud of that for ever.

Mark

All in all, 2021 was turning out to be our busiest year to date. We'd had an idea for a children's book brewing for a while. So many parents told us their kids loved the songs and played them all year round and we'd thought about creating a sausage roll character who goes on adventures.

Rox

We wanted him to be called Greg, but to be clear it had no connection to Greggs the bakery, which Mark has had an on-going but tragically unrequited love affair with his whole life. More on that later . . .

Mark

Greg doesn't realise that he's a sausage roll. In fact he's oblivious to the fact that the other characters all want to eat him. Even when he's in a perilous situation, it won't cross his mind that he's in danger.

Rox

We just wanted it to be as silly and as fun as the songs. And to try and encourage kids to enjoy reading.

Mark

Dyslexia meant that I always struggled with reading when I was younger. It's something I still struggle with now – I listen to audiobooks rather than read. Our dream was to create a book that kids like we'd been would want to pick up and enjoy.

Rox

We also wanted to create something our own kids would love and to help encourage them to find joy from reading.

Mark

Absolutely! Just because it wasn't something I'd enjoyed, I didn't want it to be the same for our boys. They were starting to show an interest in books so we wanted to help make a book they would love and be proud of.

In early 2021, following the third Christmas number one, we started pitching our idea to publishers. But we couldn't find anyone to take us on.

Rox

The feedback we kept getting was that sausage rolls weren't a healthy food so it wasn't something they wanted to promote.

Mark

But our sausage roll wasn't being eaten. It was never about him being eaten. So many publishers turned us down until we met with Puffin and they got it straight away. They loved what we'd done with the songs and bought into the vision that we had about this sausage roll character.

Rox

They put us in touch with a few illustrators and when we saw Gareth Conway's sketches, we knew that we had Greg. The picture we'd both had in our heads was staring back at us on the paper.

Mark

As with every project we take on, we also wanted to find a way to give back. Puffin had a long-standing relationship with the National Literacy Trust and it was a key part of the deal for us that for every copy of *Greg the Sausage Roll: Santa's Little Helper* sold through WHSmith, another book would be donated to a child in need.

Rox

We wanted all the pages to be bright and visual and for the illustrations to tell the story on their own in case the child wasn't able to read.

And we had big ideas for the front cover design – it should have some sparkle and stand out on the shelf from the rest of an already crowded children's book market. All of that standing our ground took courage because it was our first children's book and we didn't really know how publishing worked or whether it was 'the done thing' for authors to be so involved in the design.

But we knew what would work for Greg.

Mark

In November 2021, we went back to my old primary school in Nottingham to launch the book and it was amazing to be there. So much of it was as I remembered and it was brilliant being able to talk to the kids. They were all giving us loads of ideas for the next book, coming up with new adventures Greg could go on.

We've been to a fair few schools now with our books and kids are the best audience because they never say what you expect and they have no filter. They're the best (and also the worst, because sometimes they're very honest indeed) for market research!

Rox

Because it had a Christmas theme and it was being published during gift-buying season, we *hoped* it would do OK.

Mark

There were a whopping forty thousand pre-orders, which exceeded all expectations, and they had to get another batch printed to meet the demand.

Rox

Sales by that Christmas were well over one hundred thousand and we were sitting pretty at the top of the *Sunday Times* Bestseller List. We did a signing at Bluewater in Kent and there was a five-hour queue of people all there to see us. What was going on?!

I don't think our younger selves would ever have believed this was possible. Books could be negative, scary things for both of us growing up. They were often something to be avoided or to work a way round. And yet we've since written six more *Greg the Sausage Roll* books – that's seven bestsellers in total – and it all came from the individuality of our brains.

Mark

Whenever we do the book signings, a lot of parents of neuro-diverse children with additional needs say our book made their kids feel safe.

Rox

That honestly melts our hearts. They just love the character – he's been built for them and we protect Greg fiercely because we want to keep the magic and innocence. We own all the rights, so no one can ever mess with him.

Mark

I hope the character of Greg eventually transcends LadBaby and will still be here for generations to come, long after we've gone. What an amazing legacy that would be.

Rox

I actually feel more pressure about what we do next with Greg than what we do with LadBaby. Because he's someone kids love so much, that comes with a lot of responsibility and we really feel that on the book tours when we meet everyone.

Mark

What's so incredible about LadBaby is that people feel like they know us. And in a funny way, they kind of do. They've all seen us at home, they've seen Kobe born, they've seen us crying at the Christmas number ones. So it does feel like friendship.

Rox

People always ask after the boys, which is lovely. They remember videos from years ago and still ask about the time Mark went to register Kobe's birth and gave him the middle name Notts rather than Knox, the one we'd agreed on.

Mark

That remains one of my finest hours. At least I didn't go for Brian Clough.

Rox

If you'd done that, I'd have been straight on to divorcelawyers.com.

But it's humbling to think that people have come on this journey with us. Everyone has joined at different points and it feels like we've all known each other for ever.

Mark

We announced book seven in the *Greg* series on 5 June 2024, which was National Sausage Roll Day (always a big celebration in our house). *The World's Funniest Unicorn* was inspired by all the kids we've met over the years at signings who have told us what they'd like to see Greg do next. They wanted to see him meet a unicorn, go on a steam train . . .

Rox

. . . ride a rainbow, go on a rollercoaster . . .

Mark

. . . meet a doughnut, try candyfloss.

Rox

It was all the best things about childhood and the craziest ideas, rolled into one book.

Mark

We'd love to get *Greg* made into an animation or some sort of cartoon. But whenever we've tried, we've come up against the same barriers we did when initially pitching to get the book published. A sausage roll isn't deemed a healthy food and, so far, we've not found anyone willing to take it on.

Rox

OK, granted, Greg isn't a tomato. Or a butternut squash. But he's had multi number-one bestselling books and he was four weeks at number one for World Book Day in 2024. There's a reason kids are picking it up. They love this book and it's because they can relate to Greg.

Mark

I mean, a tiger coming to tea is surely more unhealthy for kids than a sausage roll!

Rox

A tiger who drinks all the beer and eats all the cake, no less!

Mark

Ha! Yes, mate!

With the book taking off, it was shaping up to be another jam-packed Christmas. And of course, there was a little festive sideline project with my new best mate.

Rox

Who would that be, then?

Mark

Only Ed bloody Sheeran.

13

Rocking with the Rocket Man

Rox

Of all the stark raving bonkers stuff that has happened to us over the last six years, this is probably the one I will never get my head around.

Mark

Tell me about it. What had started out as a friendly joke, ended with us in the recording studio with Sir Elton John and Ed Sheeran and putting out a single that would be our fourth Christmas number one.

Rox

How? Just…how?

Mark

It had all started way back on Christmas Day in 2020, when a message dropped into my Instagram DMs. It was from a handle I didn't recognise – @teddysphotos – but it had a blue tick, which indicated it was someone with a public profile. I opened it up.

He'd written to say how much he loves what we do at

Christmas with our songs, and that it's brought so much fun into the Christmas charts. The message went on to explain he'd delayed the release of his song, so it didn't clash with ours. He hoped we'd keep going every year and wished us Merry Christmas.

Turns out @teddysphotos was Ed Sheeran.

Rox

He was referring to the song 'Afterglow' that he'd put out on 21 December and which a lot of people had thought would derail our chances of the Christmas number one with Ronan. Ed hadn't released anything in the eighteen months before and had dropped this track as a complete surprise, so there was a lot of clamour around it.

Mark

In the end, it hadn't affected us. Just as he said in his DM, he'd released it too late to make too much of an impact on the Christmas chart.

Rox

We'd not given it another thought until we received this message. This genuine, heartfelt DM. And you can imagine that, as Mark read it out to me, I was screaming my head off.

Mark

We didn't know what to do with ourselves.

Rox

Mark has this thing whereby whenever he gets super shocked, he has to lie down on the floor. Any moment of craziness – whether it's a number one or a DM from Ed Sheeran or Elton John ringing him while he's in Sainsbury's car park (which actually happened and we'll tell you about it shortly, so hold on to your hats!) – you'll find him on the floor.

Mark

I'm literally grounding myself.

Rox

I normally join him down there and tell him it's going to be all right.

Mark

Once I'd calmed down slightly, I sent Ed a DM back:

> Hey, thank you so much for the message, it honestly means a lot. We love the opportunity to try and make people smile at Christmas and raise money for a cause that means so much to us and so many people across the UK. Love your music and can't wait to download your new song. We think it's brilliant, now it's past the cut-off time for Christmas number one! Congratulations on your first Christmas as a dad and if you ever fancy teaming up for 'Shape of Sausage Rolls', you know where we are. Merry Christmas!

And that was it. Just a little joke.

Rox

It was a bit of playful banter.

Mark

We'd done the treble; we weren't going to try for a fourth. I know we'd said that every year, but it was true. However, about halfway through 2021, we had an emotional conversation with the Trussell Trust and they asked us to please keep going.

Rox

We knew that Covid and the cost-of-living crisis meant the situation out there was only getting worse. We were regularly visiting food banks and one of the managers in Nottingham said that people would often mention LadBaby when they donated. It was through our songs that they'd learned about the charity.

She'd taken us to a basement underneath the church where they stored all the non-perishables.

This was stuff that had come in as a result of our Christmas 2020 campaign and would be distributed to people in need throughout the year.

'This is what you've done,' she said.

Mark

The awkward thing about Christmas number ones is they themselves don't make much money. That's just music in general. Unless you're Beyoncé or Drake, or Taylor Swift, you don't make a lot of money from releasing music. It's not like twenty or thirty years ago when people were buying physical copies of singles. These days with downloads and streams and YouTube, it's tough for artists.

The songs were always more of a vehicle for exposure. Of course, they raised money because people gave up their time for free and all the profits went straight to the charity, but it was the awareness the campaigns brought that really made the difference. People would hear the songs, see the publicity and donate money and food directly.

Rox

We knew the charity wanted us to go for a fourth and we'd seen the benefits for ourselves, but we were wary of overkill.

Mark

We'd seen the *X Factor* effect and how everyone had eventually got supremely fed up with them taking the Christmas number one year after year. So we said we could only go again if we felt there was a way of doing something completely different that wasn't going to annoy people. Which is when I thought I'd play my wild card. I'd message Ed and just ask the question.

Rox

Mark always has hope.

Mark

You've got to chance it. If you don't ask, you don't get.

Rox

Very true. You were bricking it, though!

Mark

I messaged him saying:

> Hey, hope you're OK. I know this is coming out of the blue and I only said it as a joke six months ago, but I'll never forgive myself if I don't ask. Is there any world in which you'd want to partner up with us at Christmas to do a song?

Rox

It took Mark about two hours to press send on that message.

Mark

I rewrote it like, forty times before I did. I remember feeling instantly embarrassed. Ed Sheeran was an international pop star, about to release his hotly anticipated fifth studio album and embark on a world tour. My little message would surely sit there in his DMs unopened. There was no way he was going to reply, not even to politely decline.

But he did. Within about thirty minutes I had a reply saying he'd love to.

Rox

We were *wetting* ourselves.

Mark

He said the only problem was that he'd already written a Christmas song with Elton John that they were doing as a duet.

He asked if we'd be up for working on it with them. They'd release their version in early December and then we'd release a second version together closer to Christmas. He said they wouldn't be offended if we said no, but that it could be a huge moment to help the charity again.

And that was another moment where I had to lie down on the floor. I must have been down there for hours this time.

Rox

Ed Sheeran and Elton John. *Elton John!* And hold on a bloody minute. *They* were asking *us* to collab with *them*? You have *got* to be joking.

Mark was mute and couldn't talk for about an hour. It was quite something. It was like he was shell-shocked. I'd never seen him like that.

But both of us knew this *had* to happen. This would elevate the charity to greater heights than we ever could on our own.

Mark

I didn't reply until the next day because I needed to do it with a calm, clear head.

> Wow. I've got to say that's literally the last thing we were expecting you to say. Thank you so much for even considering having us involved with this. Truly, it's an honour. I'm very excited because it's something that will hopefully really bring families together this Christmas and put the spotlight on food banks in a bigger way than we could have ever done. Do you think it'd be possible to jump on a call with you or your team to discuss? Honestly, my head hurts at the prospect of this happening.

Rox

Obviously it's Ed and Elton and both of their schedules were off the Richter scale, so even with the six months we had until Christmas, we were up against the clock. And I would say it was sheer panic from that moment.

Mark

This was a huge year for Ed and he had a colossal amount of promo to do around his new album, but shortly after that message exchange, we had a Zoom meeting with him and his management about how we were going to do this.

The version of the song 'Merry Christmas' he'd written and partnered with Elton on was already recorded and so he suggested we had a listen to it and then had a go at rewriting it. Only with sausage rolls.

'Um, hold on. You want us to rewrite your song?'

'Yeah,' he said. 'Just have a go! No pressure.'

No pressure?! That felt like more pressure than anything in the entire world.

Rox

They sent us over the song as an MP3 under the strict agreement that we weren't to share it anywhere. We had to sign a non-disclosure agreement holding us to that.

Mark

I remember sitting there listening to it and when it got to the end, I turned to Rox and said, 'How the f*** are we going to rewrite that?'

Rox

Those were Mark's exact words. I wish I'd taken a picture of his face, which was drained of all colour and had aged about a decade in three minutes. It was July now and we'd arranged a face-to-face session with Ed for the start of November, by which time we needed to have the bulk of the song written.

Mark

We worked on it every single night, playing the track over and over and trying to fit our lyrics in.

Rox

It was so bloody hard!

Mark

I'd say we had 80 per cent of it down on the day we went to meet Ed. It was just the last verse that we couldn't quite resolve.

Rox

We were meeting in Claridge's in London. We'd never been to Claridge's before, so it was all very exciting. They had posh mints and everything there.

Mark

We nicked the pens from the room. Still got them.

Rox

I ordered a coffee just for the craic. I had to have a Claridge's coffee, didn't I? This was all way above me.

Mark

Do you remember the guy on the door, Rox?

Rox

God yes! As we came into the lobby, the security bloke on the door – a proper south London cockney – recognised us and said, 'It's nearly Christmas time … what are you two up to?'

Mark

We just laughed and said, 'Ah, nothing, nothing!' It was still all very top secret and we hadn't wanted to jinx it by breathing a word to anyone.

Rox

We were shown to the meeting room where we were to wait for Ed to arrive. We probably wore the carpet out, pacing the floor.

Mark

Our usual cameraman Sean was with us to get some shots to cut into the video and he went to the loo and came back shaking. We asked if he was OK and he said: 'I've just had a wee next to Chris Martin. Claridge's is mad!'

Rox

The three of us were a bit doolally. But then Ed walked in, totally relaxed, with a 'Hi guys, you all right?' and gave us all hugs as if we were old mates. He was so lovely and

welcoming and seemed genuinely excited about what we
had for him.

Mark

At this point we'd still had no contact with Elton, but Ed
said he knew about everything, was up for it and was totally
involved. We'd get the song together today and once that was
sorted, he'd share it with Elton and get going.

'So, do you want to show me what you've got?' he asked.

I opened up my laptop to show him the Word document
with the lyrics we'd poured blood, sweat and tears into over
the last few months.

'Ed, this might be completely s**t ... We won't be offended
if you hate it.'

Rox

We'd kept the lyrics true to who we were. Make people laugh,
over-the-top happiness, sausage rolls. Nothing more compli-
cated than that.

Mark

I said if we'd gone too far, he had to say so.

'Mark, I'm all in!' he said. 'Make it as ridiculous as you possibly can. Whatever you want, I'll sing it. I'm here to do what
you guys do. Shall we play the song?'

Rox

OK, now this is my favourite part of the whole meeting.

Mark

Ed looked at me and said, 'Right, do you want to sing it for me?'

Did I want to sing it for him?

Rox

Hahahahaha! Excuse me while I collapse laughing. I mean no offence, Mark, but you're completely tone deaf.

Mark

'Ah now, the thing is, Ed,' I replied, 'my voice is more built for the football terraces . . .'

Rox

Dying here.

Mark

OK, Rox. Before we go any further, let's just talk some facts, shall we?

Rox

Go on.

Mark

Before we got in that meeting, just as we were walking to Claridge's, I had confided in Rox that I was having a bit of a panic that Ed was going to ask me to sing. It was my biggest fear. I said if that happened, because Rox can hold a tune, we'd hide my awful voice with her half-decent one. That would mean Rox going loud and me going quiet.

And, dear readers, let me tell you, she agreed to that wholeheartedly.

Rox

I did. I admit that. And I honestly meant it at the time.

Mark

You go loud, I'll go quiet. Those were the rules. Simple.

Fast forward to the room with Ed, the track starts playing,

he's watching me and so I have no option but to start singing. And from Rox? F***ing silence.

Rox

I couldn't even talk, let alone sing! I was watching Mark sing a sausage roll song in front of Ed Sheeran and my brain stopped functioning. Mark's face was going redder and redder and his hands were shaking.

Mark

And Ed, ever the professional, was nodding along sagely as if it was some sort of musical masterpiece. It was the most excruciating moment of my life and at no point did Rox chime in.

> Let's have a party, it's Christmas Day
> Your mum's cooking turkey
> But been moaning since yesterday
> The presents are open and the bin bags are put
> away . . .

By the second verse, he took pity on me and started singing along while I kicked Rox under the table because she'd bloody well sold me down the river.

Rox

I'm sorry! For what it's worth, I thought you did really well, babe.

Mark

We got as far as the bit we'd not managed to write and then Ed sat back in his seat.

'I love it,' he said.

Phew.

'I think it's great. It's fun, it's silly, it's exactly what it should be.'

He tweaked a couple of words in the first verse to make it scan a bit better and then he took a look at the last section, which had stumped us.

It was breathtaking to watch somebody of his talent and ability set to work. He started humming the tune and tapping the beat out on his chest and then he came up with a verse within a couple of minutes. Something we'd been tearing our hair out over for months, he had sorted in an instant and that was truly amazing to witness.

Rox

The craft was incredible. And what beauty, being able to create something so quickly. I felt so privileged that not only had we seen that happen, but we'd also had Ed Sheeran sing to us in a room. It was one of the most amazing moments I'll ever experience.

Mark

He also divided the lyrics up between us all, including Elton, in seconds, knowing instinctively what arrangement would work best. And he went away and recorded his lines at his home studio.

Rox

A couple of weeks later we hooked up with Ed again to film the video at a recording studio in Camden. By now there were rumours circulating about the collaboration and so the storyline for the video was that we were bypassing the waiting paps by smuggling Ed and Elton into the building dressed as sausage rolls.

Elton wasn't actually there that day – we were told we'd get some recording time with him in the next few weeks – but Ed put that lunatic costume on without batting an eyelid. And he spent all day with us shooting this video.

Mark

When we broke for lunch, we told Ed it was now a tradition that we ordered in a Nando's and it would be a jinx if we had anything else.

'Sure,' he said, 'I'll get this!'

We said to please let us get it as a thank you to him. And he said: 'No, honestly. I've got a black card.'

Rox

We were so starstruck by his black card. We'd heard these mythical things existed but had never seen one in real life.

Mark

He said to let his security know what we wanted and they'd go and pick it up. Could this day get any better?!

Rox

The video itself came together really well. By the end of the session, we had loads of festive content of the three of us pulling giant Christmas crackers, firing off big party cannons and wearing Elton John-style glasses. We'd also bought a couple of cheap guitars from Argos which we'd had wrapped in sausage-roll print and Ed very kindly signed them for us. It was a super-silly day.

Mark

The only issue that felt unresolved was Sir Elton. We knew he'd recently had a hip operation and there was still Covid to consider as well. We wouldn't have been surprised if his team had decided to prioritise his health instead of getting involved with all of this.

I tentatively asked Ed what the score was and he said again not to worry, it was going to happen and he'd sort it all out. I wanted to believe him.

Rox

Sure enough, about a week later, Elton John's manager emailed to say they'd heard the song so far and that he was due to record his lyrics at the Rocket studio. He would be there for an hour and would we like to come down and film with him on that day?

Mark

Of course, we said 100 per cent we'd be there. And I was terrified all over again.

Rox

It was absolutely frigging mental going into Elton John's own studio, where so many iconic songs had been recorded.

Mark

I remember seeing the number one of the building and hoping it was a sign of our future chart position.

Rox

When we went in, the place was empty apart from a security guard on the desk who directed us downstairs to the studio. There was a young lad working there and we asked why it was so quiet. He said they were moving buildings and that our song was going to be the last one ever recorded at Rocket. After that, they were packing up and going.

Holy s**t. This was history.

Mark

There was just me, Rox, our camera guy and producer and we waited in the studio for about an hour, none of us quite believing that it was going to happen.

Rox

I think our poor producer Jamie was the most scared. He was about to produce music royalty and a living legend. As a result, he was all over the place.

Mark

Elton's manager came in and spotted the plate of sausage rolls we'd set up as a prop for the video.

'Elton won't be eating a sausage roll,' she said, firmly. 'Just so you're aware.'

'That's totally fine,' I replied. 'They're more for us – would it be OK for us to hold them?'

'Yes, you can. But Elton won't be holding one.'

I told her we were going to get dressed up in Christmas jumpers and we'd brought along some Elton-inspired novelty specs (which Rox had picked up from Poundland) to wear.

'OK,' the manager said, raising an eyebrow. 'I can't promise that Elton is going to wear anything so please do manage your expectations.'

That exchange increased our existing worries because, from what she'd said, he wasn't going to be up for anything.

Rox

Suddenly, the lad who worked at the studio burst into the room to say Elton was en route. We both completely freaked out and turned into Perry from *Kevin and Perry*.

'Yes, Mrs Patterson. No, Mrs Patterson!'

He entered the room wearing a green tracksuit and I had to stop myself from curtseying.

'Hello Roxy,' he said. 'You look lovely.'

Wow, wow, wow.

Mark

He asked if we minded if he sat down because he'd not long since had this operation. And he told us he'd really been looking forward to the day.

'I think it's lovely what you do,' he said. 'Ed's told me all about it and what you'd like me to do. Give me the lyrics, I'm game!'

And then he smiled. 'We *are* going to get number one, aren't we?'

'We hope so, Elton!'

'OK, great! Let's have some fun. This is what Christmas is about, isn't it? Let's hear the song, then.'

Rox

And then Mark nearly fainted because he'd sung the first line of the track and it was about to be played for Elton.

Mark

I was just grateful that we'd already recorded our bits, so I didn't have to sing it live. But I sat there cringing myself inside out, trying to be swallowed up by my chair. Like Ed, Elton was far too polite to laugh or grimace and instead sat there all wise like the Dalai Lama, head bobbing away.

Rox

Once he'd listened to what we'd already recorded, he headed into the booth to get his lyrics down.

Mark

Elton John was about to sing the lyrics we'd written. We were stunned into a silence that was reverential. And also born out of the fact that we were all totally pooing ourselves.

> Get to the kitchen for sausage rolls
> Kids, drop your toys
> And dance along to rock and roll!

Rox

We could see him at the mic and hear him through the producer's feed. It was the weirdest feeling. These were the words we'd written in our living room.

Mark

Whenever we've recorded our songs, it takes Rox about three attempts to nail each line. It takes me about 203, that's how dreadful I am.

Elton went in there and just sang it straight off the bat first time. There was one bit where he slightly coughed mid-lyric and I remember our nervous producer asking, 'D-d-do you mind if we do that bit again, Sir Elton, please, if you don't mind thankyouplease?'

And Elton replied: 'Of course, of course! That was rubbish!'

Rox

He got everything done super quickly and then we asked if we could do some filming with him for the video. We would play the song, have a bit of a mess around and then cut the footage into what we'd already filmed with Ed.

Mark

I explained that me and Rox would be holding sausage rolls and dancing about with them.

'Well, I hope you've got me one!' he said.

We said of course and handed him a sausage roll.

'Can these be eaten or are they just props?'

'We picked them up from Greggs this morning so they can be eaten if you like!'

'OK, great!'

Rox

I went to put my snazzy Poundland specs on and Elton said, 'Are those for me?'

'I've got a whole box of them, Elton. Do you want to choose a pair?'

'Oh yeah!'

He rummaged through the box and he found a gold pair with 'Merry Christmas' written across the top. And that's what he went with.

'These really suit me!' he said.

He's worn beautiful glasses his whole life and now here he was wearing a pair of Poundland specials.

Mark

We started the camera rolling, the three of us singing along to the song and Elton tucking into his sausage roll all the way through!

Rox

He was holding my hand and swaying along and just seemed so happy to be involved. We loved him to pieces.

Mark

There's a clip right at the end of the video that we left in where he says, 'I haven't had a sausage roll in years ... story of my life at the moment!'

And then he mentioned to his manager about needing to get to Greggs to buy some sausage rolls in.

Rox

We'd been told we would only have an hour with Elton, but it had been easily double that by the time he said goodbye. He told us that anything we needed, just to ask his team.

'I've got every faith in you,' he said. 'I'm here to support you, but you guys have got this. This is your song. This is your campaign.'

It was the most incredible day ever.

Mark

We left there on such a high. Which made what happened next all the more painful. There was a whole world of trouble brewing that would completely blindside us, wreaking havoc on our lives. We had no idea of the chaos and anguish about to hit.

14

Under Attack

Mark

What became the toughest time of our lives happened out of nowhere. As we write this book in 2024, more than three years on since the rug was pulled from under us, it's something we are still suffering the fallout from. I'm not ashamed to say that it took an immense toll on my mental health.

Rox

This is the first time we've ever spoken about it. I don't think either of us has felt ready to do that until now because the impact was too great and the emotions too raw.

But as we promised you right at the beginning, we want to lay everything bare in this book and tell our story how it is. How we've seen it, felt it and lived it.

Mark

It began on 10 December 2021, when we revealed the big secret and publicly announced the collaboration with Ed and Elton. 'Sausage Rolls for Everyone' (our version of 'Merry Christmas') would be released the following week and was aiming for the Christmas number one, again with all the profits going to the Trussell Trust. We had a load of media lined up, including an appearance on *The One Show* on the day of release, which was a real coup and would be awesome for the campaign.

We were so excited about what the next couple of weeks had in store.

Rox

But there came a backlash so quick and so severe that it was like a punch to the face. It seemed to be getting stirred up by a singer/songwriter guy we'd never heard of. We'd rather not mention his name in this book because of the pain he caused us, or give him that platform because he doesn't deserve to be talked about. However, for context, he had a political anti-establishment and extremely sweary protest song due for release on the same day as us.

Mark

As far as I'm aware, immediately after our announcement of the collab with Ed and Elton, he put out a video across his socials, trying to whip up some anti-LadBaby feeling to stop us getting to number one. That basically gave people licence to come at us and we started being bombarded with the most vile posts across all our channels.

We'd had the odd sh**ty comment in the past but nothing more than that – I would always say how lucky we were that we'd never had to suffer the trolling we'd hear about from other creators. We'd always had good press and good relationships within the media, mainly because we took such care with our content. It was always wholesome, family-centred fun with no swearing, and we never strayed into controversial or contentious waters.

But suddenly we were getting messages that came from a place of pure malice and there was so much of it. It was the first time we'd experienced anything like this and it hit us like a truck.

Rox

The abuse was overwhelming. Every time we posted anything, there would be a deluge of horrible, personal comments underneath. They would range from nasty, personal remarks about our looks to out-and-out hatred. Some people really, really despised us and didn't mind letting us know. Twitter was especially vicious and we eventually came off there completely. Poison.

Because this had never happened to us before, we didn't know what to do or how to stop it. We felt helpless.

Mark

It's hard to describe what it's like to find yourself in the eye of an internet troll storm, but it feels inescapable. Like a pressure cooker. I started having sleepless nights, too stressed to do anything but lie awake. I'd block the worst offenders, but it was like whack-a-mole. I'd get rid of one and then five more would appear.

Rox

After a few days of this, I was in the playground with the kids and I must have been in quite a heightened state. Mark had just had a rough night as he tried to grapple with this barrage of abuse and something inside me snapped. That was quite unusual for me, but I was sleep-deprived, anxious and juggling too many plates. I'd had enough.

I filmed a video addressing some of the negativity we were experiencing, hoping that people would watch it and see that this was very real for us and maybe, just maybe, they'd think twice before posting.

How naive I was.

Mark

Our strategy (if you want to call it that) was not to respond. Ignore, ignore, ignore. Engaging would surely only add fuel to the fire and our hope was that all this would blow over once the trolls got bored and moved on to the next target.

Rox

Only it didn't blow over. In fact, it had barely even started.

Mark

The Official Charts called and asked if we could do an interview about going for number one again and of course I said yes. Even though I was feeling a bit wobbly after more than a week of dealing with these attacks, I never turned down opportunities to amplify the charity campaign and hopefully notch up a few more sales in the process.

During that interview, I was asked about the competition for the top spot and we had a bit of a discussion about Mariah and Wham! and how much fun it was to go up against them again.

And then the journalist asked, 'What do you think about the anti-government song?'

I answered truthfully and said I didn't know a huge amount about the song, but that it didn't sound like it was in the spirit of Christmas, which was a time for kids and families.

'It takes a certain sort of person to download a song with that much swearing in the title,' I said, 'but you never know. There's definitely an element that people aren't happy with this government, but our song is for charity ... and ours is trying to raise more money than ever for food banks. It's something that is even more important given everything that is going on.'

That was my honest take on it and I thought I'd managed to navigate the question, answer fairly diplomatically and steer it back to our message. But when the interview went live the next day, it all kicked off.

The person spearheading this had dug around and found a two-year-old, long-forgotten interview I'd done with the *Guardian* back in 2019, right after the second number one. I remember the record label PR had set it up, telling me that the writer wanted to focus on food banks and why we supported the Trussell Trust.

'Having said that,' she'd warned, 'it's the *Guardian* so they might try and get you on politics.'

This was a week or so after the 2019 general election, which had seen Prime Minister Boris Johnson return a huge Conservative majority.

'Just try and avoid getting into that if you can.'

Rox

That was fine by us. As a rule, we never talk politics or religion because that's not what our platform is for.

Mark

I was just a bloke trying to help raise money for food banks, I wasn't trying to overthrow the government. That's not to say that I don't have opinions! I've always followed the news and am very conscious of the world around me, but it's never been my place to discuss politics publicly.

Anyway, sure enough, the *Guardian* journalist had asked me what I thought about the fact the Conservatives had just been voted back in. I'd tried to skirt around it by saying that the only government able to effect change was the one in power and since the public had voted for the Tories, we had to hope they would now do the right thing by the nation.

She'd pushed me a little, asking me who I'd voted for and I'd replied that while yes, I *had* voted, I'd prefer not to say who for.

And two years later, that was all the 'evidence' he needed.

He posted that old interview and started putting it about that, 'LadBaby's a Tory, he voted Tory, the Tories are the reason food banks exist and LadBaby voted them in.'

Rox

He accused us of using the food banks 'to hawk records' and gain 'lucrative sponsorship deals'.

And, most despicably of all, to 'bolster' our bank balance. He was saying we were profiting from the charity singles. None of it was true. Not one bit.

Mark

Of everything said during that time, it was the accusation that we'd been making money from the songs that killed me. It was such a kick in the gut because it wasn't true. But it was an untruth that took hold and then spun out of control online.

Rox

To this day I have sadness in my heart about what that guy did. We never made a penny from the songs; we never even claimed expenses. All the way through our Christmas number-one campaigns, we had done the right thing and kept the charity at the forefront.

Everything he said was absolute f***ing bulls**t, but people believed it and, as it gathered pace, we felt too overwhelmed to defend ourselves. We didn't even know how to.

Mark

For total transparency, we always said it was 'one hundred per cent of the profits', rather than 'proceeds' because, legally, that's what you *have* to say. It's profits as opposed to proceeds because whenever you record any song there are functional costs that have to come out to go to the likes of Spotify, iTunes and Amazon and to cover distribution.

Rox

We always asked them to waive their fees, but they never did.

Mark

I can't tell iTunes they're not allowed to take a percentage. We were using their platform. They take a percentage from every song on there, not just ours. Once all functional costs had been covered, the rest of the money went directly to the Trussell Trust from the record label.

None of the money ever came to me or Rox. We gave up all of our time for free and we feel honoured and privileged to have been in a position to do that.

Rox

There was some nonsense conspiracy theory flying around that only 7 per cent went to the charity because we were syphoning off the rest. Again, to be absolutely crystal clear, me and Mark have never taken any money from any of the songs.

Mark

As we said earlier, we even switched off all monetisation on our channels for the period over Christmas. We would turn down lucrative offers from brands during that time because it didn't feel right to be promoting products when the focus should be on food banks and the charity. But nobody cared about the facts. They preferred to revel in trolling us over something concocted online.

And the ironic thing is, I'd voted Labour in the 2019 general election. I've always voted Labour.

Rox

We were both brought up in Labour-supporting families.

Mark

We grew up in working-class households where voting Labour was a given. I've voted Labour at every local and general election. I voted Remain in the 2016 EU referendum.

Rox

We are not Tories!

Mark

I wish now that I'd just said that at the time. But hindsight is wonderful and we thought by refusing to engage, we would help dial it down. Online arguments, especially around politics, rarely end well and it was the reason we'd never crossed that line in the past.

Rox

I was permanently on edge and felt extremely unsafe. We'd hear people in the street saying, 'Look it's those f***ing dick-heads', and then whisper about 'the charity money'. Me and Mark aren't confrontational in the slightest, so we would never get into a back and forth with anyone. We'd much rather walk away as quickly as possible, especially if the kids are with us.

We were getting threatening DMs and emails saying, 'We know where you live', and I started not wanting to leave the house because I knew that there were people who believed what they'd read and seemed willing to lash out at us.

Mark

There were messages from people saying if they ever saw me round Nottingham, they were going to stab me.

A kid came up to me during a Nottingham Forest home game and asked me to sign his copy of *Greg the Sausage Roll*, which of course I was more than happy to do.

Unbeknown to me, someone sitting a few rows back had

filmed this encounter and then posted it on Twitter saying: 'Look at this f***ing tw*t. He really thinks he's a some-body now.'

And then all the comments underneath were like, 'Tell me where he sits, I know what he's f***ing up to, he's that f***er who steals from charity, what seat number is he?' and it became terrifying very quickly.

I'd sat in the same seat since I was a kid and now I wasn't sure if it was safe for me to return.

Rox

I'd get DMs saying, 'I've seen your husband going home, I'm going to follow him and kill him.' Obviously we reported all this to the police, we took screenshots and uploaded everything we had to a USB stick, which we then handed over.

Mark

Nottinghamshire Police came to see us on New Year's Eve and told us they'd taken a look at everything we'd shared with them but there was nothing they could do.

Rox

With no one to pin this on, they had nothing. And even if they'd managed to identify who was behind it, they weren't even sure what charges we'd be able to bring.

In the end I had to stop reading the comments for my own sanity. I needed to be mentally right for the children and I couldn't take it.

Mark

Rox stopped looking, but I couldn't help myself. I read everything.

Rox

I don't know how you did it, love. You were so strong for us.

Mark

Every comment, every message, every email. I felt like I needed to stay across this and know exactly what was going on and what people were saying.

Reading the comments was something I'd always done anyway. I did it to stay in tune with what people made of our videos and we've always been reactive to feedback and what followers thought and wanted us to do next. So in a way, I couldn't *not* read them, even though I knew it was making everything ten times worse. People were saying things like, 'LadBaby's team must be working overtime with all the deleting and blocking', but it was only ever me on my own. There was no team. It was just me, wading through the bile and blocking people left, right and centre.

Rox

We've always had quite a strict trolling policy in place on our channels that means we block anyone being hateful. Because we're a family and it's other families who follow us, we just get rid of any nastiness or negativity. We also have all the four-letter words restricted so no one can post anything sweary and our philosophy is, if you've been horrible, you're not welcome.

Mark

And that had always worked well for us. The thing is, I don't mind somebody expressing an opinion. I've never blocked people who say, 'I don't like this' or 'This is boring.' Fair enough, that's a bit rude, but they're entitled to say it and I'll leave them be.

It's the abusive comments that earned the block, and they were relentless.

And when you're in the thick of it, you only see the bad stuff. I know now there were ten times as many of our followers arguing back and defending us, but I wasn't focusing on that.

There could be hundreds of positive comments, but I'd only see ones attacking us.

It was the worst time of my life. We were being accused of something we hadn't done, but denying it seemed to make it even worse. If we tried to set the record straight during an interview (because the accusations had cut through and now it was a question that came up in every single one), it just gave the trolls another lease of life.

We were very conscious not to get dragged into a war of words with anyone, which was exactly what they wanted and would have been playing into their hands. We were advised to focus on the song, keep stressing it was 100 per cent of profits to the Trussell Trust and ride it out.

Rox

Which was impossible to do. It dominated our every moment, our every thought.

There were probably fewer than fifty accounts who were actively trolling us twenty-four-seven, but they were tireless and it felt suffocating. For many of them it became a vendetta.

Mark was so crushed by it all that I genuinely worried about him having a stroke. I know that might sound like an over-reaction, but the stress was seriously affecting him and he was taking most of the burden by reading all the comments to protect me and the boys. I was petrified for him.

Mark

I started having panic attacks. They would normally be trig-gered if I was due to do an interview. These were interviews I wanted to do to raise awareness for the Trussell Trust, but I'd work myself up into a state where my chest would tighten and I couldn't breathe.

I'd never experienced anything like that before. When I was at school, I used to worry a lot and get stressed about exams, but it wasn't like this and I'd certainly not felt this level of anxiety as an adult. I tried to stay focused on what we were doing, but the terror was overpowering at times.

Rox

It was like a growing cult of people who would home in on everything we did and wanted to end us. It was heartbreaking when we knew we'd not done anything wrong and all we'd ever wanted was to try and do some good at Christmas, but it felt like no one believed us. It wasn't only unfair, it wasn't true either.

We tried to take comfort in the fact that our audience were loyal and would know that it was all lies. The Trussell Trust reached out to us to check we were OK, which was good of them.

Mark

We were managing ourselves and so we had no 'team' to cocoon us or advise us on how to deal with the attacks.

Rox

Because we'd never responded to anything negative in the past and had always stuck to our values and carried on, that's what we resolved to do here. But it's unreal how quickly fake news travels and can take hold with such devastating consequences.

We were feeling quite traumatised by it all, which made it impossible to think straight. The trolls were in control and there were more of them, so whatever we said, we'd be on the back foot. I was living in a perpetual state of fear because I knew it would only take one angry, misinformed person to see us in the street and hurt us.

Even people we'd been friendly with online pulled away and distanced themselves.

Mark

I did start to wonder if we were over. Was this the end?

Rox

Me too. It felt like the beginning of being effectively cancelled.

Mark

I don't think we ever lost any contracts, thankfully. We'd worked with a lot of the brands for quite a while by now and they knew us and trusted us.

And they had the good sense to know that we weren't going to get Ed Sheeran and Elton John to work with us on a song if we were stealing the money. The Trussell Trust wouldn't have had anything to do with us over all those years if we were scam artists.

There was never any concern about the money from either the Ed or the Elton camps. They were across everything; they knew the deal and they were happy with the contract between the Trussell Trust and the record label.

But there was this horrible perception of us that was spreading like wildfire, all from a rumour that had been pieced together very carefully to attack us.

Rox

God, yeah. It definitely changed us. We're positive people and always try to see the sunny side of life. I've always been a super-confident, outgoing, bubbly person. But this was way too much for even the strongest of characters to withstand.

Even on the school run, I stopped interacting with people because I was so mortified by what was happening. We were also very frightened about how the boys might be affected or targeted and at one point I wanted to take them out of school.

Mark

We spoke to the school and explained how much abuse we were getting and how worried we were about the boys' safety. I suppose that fear tells you where our heads were at that time.

Rox

We were trapped in an anxious bubble and existing only in survival mode.

Mark

We just had to get to Christmas. Get through this campaign, keep in mind why we were doing it and know that's all that mattered.

Rox

We had truth and facts on our side. That was worth so much more than the gossip and the rumours. We couldn't escape the trolling, but we could put the blinkers on and focus on the end game.

Mark

We didn't think we had any chance of getting to number one now, but we were more concerned about whether all this had damaged the reputation of a good cause. Were people going to stop believing in charity campaigns as a whole? Were they going to lose faith in donating if they thought that's what happened to their money?

Rox

I kept thinking of those kids I'd met. Those mums who just wanted to feed their families. And the fear that this lie was going to impact on the help they were getting was probably the worst pain I've ever felt.

Mark

Me too. However, against all expectations, on Christmas Eve 2021 we were announced as the number one again. But it was such a bittersweet moment.

Rox

We had the euphoria of equalling the Beatles' record of four consecutive Christmas number ones. But it was tempered by a huge sense of 'thank god that's over' and then the anxiety of what now lay ahead.

Mark

And, in fact, getting the number one only elevated the abuse. It should have been cause for celebration and yet it was unbearable to process. The coverage in the press, the awareness for the charity, the fantastic public support and the honour of working with Ed Sheeran and Sir Elton John made it beyond anything we'd ever done before. But the abuse that came with it was intolerable.

Maybe the fact it had become so big and the spotlight had become so bright meant that we attracted more trolls. Maybe the success had opened us up to this.

Rox

Even thinking about it now feels like I'm reliving it and it makes me really breathless.

Mark

Other than each other, we didn't talk to anybody about it. We didn't want to worry our families or be judged by anyone outside of that. It felt totally isolating.

Rox

It was a very scary, lonely place to be.

Mark

In the middle of this crisis, there were some rare lighter moments. Ones we still cherish today. On Christmas Day, the day after we'd been announced as the number one, Ed rang us and we jumped on a Zoom with him, which was amazing.

Rox

The fact he'd taken time out to do that on Christmas Day meant the world to us, when everything else was in such turmoil. Kobe was running through the house naked during the call – that's definitely one to tell him about when he's older.

Mark

We mentioned to Ed that we'd not heard from Elton but just wanted to check he was happy. Ed said that he knew he had our number and that he'd been meaning to call us – he would follow up and see what was happening. Anyway, shortly after that, we got an email from Elton's manager asking to double check my mobile number.

Rox

Between Christmas and New Year, I sent Mark to Sainsbury's to do a top-up shop.

Mark

And it was as I was getting back to the car that my phone started ringing from an unknown number. I answered, expecting it to be someone from the media wanting an interview.

'Hello, darling,' boomed the instantly recognisable voice on the end of the line. 'It's Elton!'

Argh!

'Er, hello, Elton! How are you?'

'I'm *fantastic*! I can't believe we did it. Number one! It's going to make such a difference – congratulations.'

I thanked him and said we were relieved to hear he was happy and how much it had meant to us to have him involved.

'The strangest thing has been happening,' he said. 'I've left you four or five voicemails over the last few days. Turns out, it wasn't your number! So somebody somewhere has a load of voicemails from me!'

I mean, can you imagine that person? The thought of them listening to these messages and not knowing why the hell Elton John was calling them is pure brilliance.

Rox

We were in touch with Ed Sheeran a lot over that festive period, too, and one day in the run-up to Christmas, he'd said he had a present for Mark.

Mark

He reached into his wallet, took out his Greggs black card and handed it to me. First Nando's and now Greggs! When you reach Ed Sheeran levels of fame and success, you must get black cards for every major food chain. Forget the number-one albums, adoring fans and sell-out international tours: this is what it's all about!

Rox

Just touching it sent Mark into a spin.

Mark

I told him I couldn't accept it.

'Of course you can!' he said. 'It's morally wrong for me to have one of these things and not you. Take it!'

And who was I to turn him down? Free sausage rolls for life!

Two days later, I thought I'd try it out. I popped into Greggs in Nottingham and handed over the card to pay for a sausage roll.

The assistant looked at it and then looked at me.

'We can't accept this,' she said.

'Oh, um, why's that?'

'It's got Ed Sheeran's name on it.'

Foiled.

Rox

Then Greggs got in touch.

Mark

We'd recorded a video with Ed to show the gifting of the black card and Greggs responded with a private message telling us that they had seen that news and calling Ed a 'great guy' but said 'Unfortunately, this card is specifically for Ed, not you. It is only for Ed to use when he's on the UK leg of his global tour.' We were gutted. They finished by saying, 'If you're ever going on a global tour, we would be happy to discuss a black card with you.'

Rox

The shade! It feels like they don't like us.

Mark

Greggs have never wanted to team up with us. I've approached them a few times saying we'd love to work with them and create something fun, but only ever received a very corporate email back stating that as a brand they don't look to partner with celebrities or influencers.

Anyway, I replied to their message saying it was a shame to hear that the card wasn't valid for me. I wasn't going on a tour but it would be great if they wanted to donate anything to the Trussell Trust and if they ever wanted to work on something more meaningful, I'd love to team up with them.

I've heard nothing since.

Rox

Their loss, babe.

Mark

By the time January came around, we were worn out, mentally and emotionally. We needed to look at the New Year as a reset, a chance to pick ourselves up creatively and rebuild. We wanted to get back to doing what we loved, but it was an odd place to be and everything felt uncertain.

Rox

One thing I was sure of was that there was no way we could do a fifth single. We had both gone through a trauma and I knew I wouldn't be able to face that for a second time. I couldn't see Mark suffer again, either.

We would continue to support the charity but from behind closed doors. I didn't want anyone to have the opportunity to question our morals or our motives.

Mark

The trolling had definitely peaked and things started to die down. But although it was no longer a torrent, there was still a steady stream of nasty comments. Like a constant murmur. Some bloke had gone to the effort of making a video trawling through our accounts on Companies House and speculating over where he thought we made our money.

By this point we'd been making videos for five years. We'd worked with brands like Disney and McDonald's, we had YouTube and Facebook revenues with a subscription zone, Rox had a sell-out clothing line, we'd written a number-one bestselling book. That was where our income came from.

But as far as he was concerned, all the money we earned was from the charity songs. It was ludicrous, but then that video got shared and did the rounds so it never really went away.

Rox

I was desperate to settle down and get back to normal. Comedy and entertainment were where our hearts were and so we knuckled down. I think our first video after Christmas was a couples' challenge, which was well received and gave us both a boost. Our audience was still with us.

Mark

But while the attacks had subsided, my anxiety remained. The panic attacks continued and they are something I still battle today. I'm getting better at recognising the triggers now, but once they start, I can't stop them and I just have to wait for them to pass. At their worst, they can be completely debilitating.

Rox

You were so broken. It was no way to live and this was precisely why I said we had to walk away from the Christmas singles. No more. We had to prioritise our health and our family and stop.

Mark

And I agreed wholeheartedly. But . . .

Rox

But?

Mark

But then we got an email from the Band Aid Charitable Trust.

Rox

I said not to do it. It would leave us wide open to further attacks and I didn't have the capacity to cope.

Mark

I thought it would too. I knew it would.

Rox

And it did. Only this time it would be far, far worse than we could possibly have anticipated.

15

The Worst is Yet to Come

Mark

It was an incredibly disorientating position to find ourselves in. On one hand, to be involved in a project that remains the professional achievement we're most proud of. But on the other, to be wondering if it was something we should never have started.

Rox

We will never regret the work we've done for charity. Never ever. But we have definitely questioned why on earth we pressed ahead with the fifth Christmas campaign. Our heads were screaming, 'For the love of Christ, don't do it!'

But our hearts . . .

Mark

. . . our hearts said something different. In February 2022, we received that email from the Band Aid Charitable Trust.

Rox

Actual Band Aid!

Mark

The real deal. It was written by John Kennedy, who is one of the trustees, and he said they'd been watching what we'd been doing for the last four years and we should be very proud. He added that on the back of our campaigns, he and some of the other trustees had donated to the Trussell Trust.

Rox

When it comes to charity songs, Band Aid is the first one everyone thinks of. They were the OGs! The pioneers who had started what we were doing now.

We'd been so battered and bruised by what had happened over Christmas and New Year and getting an email like that restored my faith a bit. Because we *should* be proud. And, like us, there were good people out there doing good things.

Mark

John didn't know it, but his email was a kind of validation. No matter what the trolls were saying, the right people believed in us and what we were doing. So I replied, thanking John and saying it was an honour to receive a message from him.

Rox

What did you write next, Mark?

Mark

Well. I think I said something very tongue in cheek along the lines of, 'Imagine if we all got together and did a song?!'

Rox

Breathe, Rox. Breathe.

Mark

And the response came back within thirty minutes: 'We'd love to! Let's do it.'

It appeared that I'd just signed us up to do another one.

Rox

I thought he was on the wind-up when he told me.

Mark

I'd said it flippantly, not expecting them to say yes, a bit like what happened with Ed.

But now it felt like an opportunity too big to turn down. We'd thought Ed and Elton would be impossible to top, but this would be teaming up with the people behind the biggest charity song in history and would undoubtedly take the campaign up another level. Profits would be shared equally between Band Aid and the Trussell Trust.

Rox

That was the thought process and it was hard to argue against it, despite my worries about history repeating itself with the trolling. And what nailed it for both of us was getting Sir Bob Geldof's seal of approval.

Mark

I asked John Kennedy if it would be OK to rewrite the lyrics to 'Do They Know It's Christmas?' and he replied saying he'd spoken to Sir Bob who had given the go-ahead.

Rox

Whoa. So now we were writing sausage roll lyrics for the biggest charity song in history with Sir Bob's blessing. Part of me was like: 'Do you know what? F*** it. Let's just go for it.'

I felt like we had nothing to lose. We'd already been through the worst that could be thrown at us and the best response to that was surely to carry on putting good out there.

Gah! I'd talked myself into it.

Mark

At least this time we would be going into it with our eyes wide open. And if people saw that Band Aid trusted us, then maybe speculation about us being 'thieves' and pocketing the money would dissipate. That wasn't the reason we signed up, but at the back of my mind I hoped it might be a by-product of the partnership.

Rox

And, in a nutshell, that's how we ended up doing the one thing we'd vowed never to do again.

It was a tough one to get together this time. Our initial plan was to form a Band Aid supergroup, just as they had done for the 1984, 1989, 2004 and 2014 singles, and we started making approaches to various celebrities and artists.

Mark

But we couldn't get anyone to do it. No one was up for it. I would send countless DMs on Instagram and our record label told us they were reaching out to the biggest names in the music industry via their agents and PR teams, but nothing was happening. The handful of replies we did get were only to ask who else had signed up. We'd respond that it was early stages, but we were getting in touch with the biggest names in the music industry ... and that would be the last we'd hear from them.

Rox

Come on, Mark, let's talk about some of the people who apparently nearly happened. A list had been drawn up of who the record label was going after.

Mark

We were told Stormzy was too busy, Lewis Capaldi was having a break from music due to his mental health and Bono's team wanted to see who else would be on the track first. Apparently Kylie Minogue, Craig David and Paul McCartney were all being called via a record label contact.

Rox

Can you imagine if we'd actually got Kylie Minogue?! I think I would have died.

Mark

There was even supposedly someone within the record label who had links to speak with Adele because they shared lawyers.

Rox

OMG I CAN'T COPE. Adele. Actually Adele. That is my dream. She's probably one of three people who we wished we'd had the chance to do a Christmas song with. Adele, Michael Bublé and Mariah Carey.

Mark

Agreed! Music and Christmas royalty. Randomly the only person who came close was James Blunt. We'd been told he loved the idea and wanted to be part of it, but when we weren't able to secure any more talent his team stopped responding to our emails.

Rox

We'd told the Trussell Trust that Band Aid had approached us and given permission to use the song, and they were overjoyed and excited to see who we were going to get on board. So we did feel pressure to turn this into something amazing.

Mark

I don't know whether people were aware of the trolling and abuse but maybe there was now a question mark over us. Perhaps people thought we were tainted and didn't want to be 'guilty by association', so best to play safe and not come near.

Rox

The supergroup plan wasn't going to work and so we had to start thinking creatively about how we could do it differently.

Mark

And that's when we thought about using celebrity lookalikes. We'd actually had a funny idea around lookalikes for a couple of years and now seemed like the best time to deploy it! We wrote the lyrics and then contacted a load of agencies, lining up all these 'celebs' to film the video at Dean Street Studios.

Rox

It turned out to be comedy gold with all these hilarious interactions between them.

Mark

We had Robbie chatting up Kylie Minogue and Elton breaking up a fight between Liam and Noel. Oh, Adele with her glass of wine!

Rox

OMFG, the Paul McCartney in his Karen wig!

Mark

Paul McCartney was the only one we didn't book, he just turned up on the day! He walked in and we were like, 'Who's that?' because, let's be real, he was stretching the definition of the word 'lookalike'.

Rox

The Liam and Noel were such brilliant sports. They knew each other from the lookalike circuit and were good mates, but as soon as the cameras started rolling they'd assume their characters and argue over ridiculous things. It was as if they morphed into the Gallaghers and it was hilarious to watch.

Mark

The Elton John was a cab driver and such a character. Our Robbie was incredible. He sounded just like him.

Rox

And we had a *real-life* Martin Lewis, of course.

Mark

Who doesn't love Martin Lewis? Everyone loves Martin Lewis! He's the nation's official Money Saving Expert and when he talks you stop and listen. He's captivating and a trusted pair of hands and having him involved was the curveball no one saw coming. We'd contacted him and explained that we had this joke in mind for the video where Rox thought we were recording with Lewis Capaldi, but it's another Lewis – Martin – who turns up.

And he loved it. He came back very quickly and was up for it.

Rox

It was such a fun, energetic, feelgood day of filming and recording and everyone was buzzing for the charity. It felt as exciting as it had been for the very first one back in 2018, and perhaps the high of that day in the studio gave us a false sense of security.

We probably should have known what was coming.

Mark

When the song was announced, the abuse blew up all over again, only this time it was even more vitriolic and seething with hate, and the focus of a lot of the attacks was on Martin Lewis. People were piling in on him and asking how he could associate himself with us. It was the same accusations as last year: we were Tories, we were profiting from the songs and he was a hypocrite for having anything to do with us.

The same social media accounts who had been making our lives hell for the last year were now going at him. He appeared to be extremely shocked and shaken by it.

Rox

I don't know if he'd ever experienced anything like this before and it can be devastating to deal with.

Mark

He did. He came to us and asked what was going on and we were very honest. As we had done at the beginning, we showed him everything we had to prove that we weren't taking anything and that the money all went to the charity.

He was lovely about it, but it felt like he was also at a complete loss as to how to respond to the attacks – he'd tried politely replying to a few comments saying there was no obligation to buy the single and suggesting people just donate directly to the Trussell Trust instead – but it wasn't touching the sides.

Rox

They just kept on coming for him. Us, too.

Mark

It wasn't just contained to the internet. We started getting shouted at in the street and the supermarket. One of the most horrific incidents happened when we were out in Nottingham with the kids at a pop-up Christmas market.

We found some silly slogan Christmas jumpers and I asked the stallholder if he had any in a larger size.

'Not for you,' he said.

'I'm sorry?' I replied.

'You f***ing stole from a charity.'

'What are you on about, mate?'

'I f***ing know. And I'm not selling you nothing!'

Rox

He was full of hate and aggression, and Phoenix and Kobe saw and heard all of this happen. We walked away in shock.

Mark

My anxiety was through the roof and I was having daily panic attacks. My chest would tighten and I'd struggle to breathe, like I wasn't capable of taking in enough air. Sometimes it would pass very quickly and other times it would go on for several hours.

Rox

When he's recovering from an attack, Mark shuts down. He lies down on the sofa and it's almost as if he passes out from the stress and exhaustion of what's just happened to him.

Mark

A few days into the campaign, Martin invited me on to *Good Morning Britain*, where he was presenting that week.* I got a cab down to London the evening before and I had a panic attack the whole way there. When I got to the hotel I couldn't sleep.

By the time I got to the studio the following morning, I was a nervous wreck. I saw Martin before we went live and I don't think he was in a great place, either.

He said to me: 'I don't understand all this abuse aimed at me. Did you know this was going to happen?'

I told him that we'd had it pretty bad last year but hadn't

---

* *Good Morning Britain*, ITV1, 14 December 2022

thought it would explode like this and especially not as it was being done with Band Aid.

He explained that he had no choice but to address the money claims on the show and made it clear that I would have to say publicly that we weren't earning anything from the songs.

'Martin,' I said, 'please feel free to ask me what you want to. We've never taken any money, so I'm more than happy to say that.'

Rox

He'd wanted to know what exact percentage from the sales would go to the charity after Apple, Spotify and Amazon had taken their standard industry costs, along with any of the other functional costs implicated with making, recording and distributing a song. But it's impossible to put a figure on that until all the downloads and streaming numbers are in because there are so many factors at play.

Mark

The percentage one single stream counts towards one single unit sale in the charts also differs if the listener is paying for a subscription on a music streaming service or if they're playing it for free on something like YouTube.

Rox

None of this was possible to know and wasn't information we had to give him.

Mark

We had spoken to our legal team and the record label, and the most simple and factual answer was: 'One hundred per cent of profit goes to the charity.'

Rox

Mark wanted the focus to be on the song so we could raise money and awareness for the charity, but instead the allegations made by the trolls against Martin and us were taking over and becoming the main story.

Mark

He was hosting with Kate Garraway who was lovely, probably because she was removed from it and saw it a bit differently. But Martin was hurting.

He tried to push me to say live on air that this was definitely the last single.

'We're telling everyone right now, there will be no more,' he said. It felt like an ambush.

As I was about to stumble over my answer, Kate jumped in and said: 'Well it surely depends if the food bank situation gets worse? It's not that they *want* to keep coming back. They're doing it to help food banks.'

And that rescued me because Martin had put me on the spot.

Rox

Mark came home from that TV appearance emotionally drained. He went to lie on the sofa. He couldn't eat or really communicate.

For the next few days, he alternated between sleeping and waking up to edit a video or check in with the charity. That was all he was able to do; it was like he was on autopilot.

Mark

Clearly under enormous pressure and shaken by the harassment, Martin distanced himself from the entire project following that interview.

Rox

He had to protect himself and thought the best way to do that was to step back. We respected that. He probably felt his career was on the line. His reputation has to stay squeaky clean for him to retain people's trust, I suppose. And I know going through that sort of trolling is horrific.

Mark

He never blamed us and he didn't explicitly withdraw his support, but he obviously felt he could no longer be actively involved. That was a huge shame, but I got it.

He never contacted us again after that and we've not spoken to him since. And that broke my heart because I love Martin Lewis and it was such a wonderful partnership which had made so much sense. We will be for ever grateful that he decided to be part of the project but we were gutted that it did not grow into something bigger between us. We'd spoken at length on the video shoot about how much he loved what we were doing and was a massive supporter of using social media to spread a positive message and help important causes.

Rox

Didn't it feel like he wanted to work with you again in a more meaningful way?

Mark

Yeah. I'm gutted that never happened. I thought there would be an opportunity for us to work together on TV. A way to join our social media presence with a TV audience to help further support struggling families. But it didn't happen.

Rox

We had to drive the boat on the song from that point on and, god, it was brutal. Martin was still on all the promotional imagery, but we had to go it alone and the song hadn't even been released yet.

The night before 'Food Aid' was released, one of the boys had a febrile convulsion in the middle of the night. Any parent who has experienced that will know that it's completely terrifying and we had to call an ambulance.

Mark

This was at about 3 a.m. and we were due to be leaving at six to drive to Manchester to do a live TV interview on *BBC Breakfast* and then a full day in a BBC radio studio doing regional radio interviews over fifteen locations across the UK.

Rox

I was all over the place emotionally. I was with a very poorly little boy who had been rushed to hospital, but I was also scared for Mark who was so stressed out and mentally unwell that I thought he was going to have a nervous breakdown or a heart attack and was now having to travel to Manchester solo.

Mark

I felt I had to keep going because the opportunity to talk about the Trussell Trust to so many people was too important to miss and we needed to drive as much awareness to the charity and the single as possible. But the abuse was only ramping up and we'd be verbally attacked in the street.

Rox

We were frightened. We even paid for security to go to Alton Towers with us around that time. It was an organised event, but we were getting so much abuse that we didn't dare go to such a public place without protection.

Mark

If it had been the two of us we'd have maybe risked it without security. But we were taking the kids and it was more out of worry for them than ourselves.

Rox

Then Mark had to stop going to the football because of two scary incidents.

Mark

The first had happened inside the City Ground with a bloke who was quite drunk and asking for a photo. It had seemed good-natured at first but then he turned.

'I saw you last week and asked for a photo and you f***ing ignored me,' he said.

'Mate, I've never turned down a photo in my life if somebody wants it. Happy to do one now if you want?'

'Nah, I don't want one with you anyway now after what you f***ing do with charity money. I know all about that.'

He wasn't in the right frame of mind, shall we say, to discuss things rationally. This wasn't the sort of situation that was going to be salvaged with a civil conversation, so I walked away, quite spooked.

Rox

Thank god you did. That was the right thing to do.

Mark

But then there was something else more serious. It was after a home game and I was in the pub around the corner from the ground with my mates. As I was queuing for the toilet, there was a bloke behind me and he said: 'It's you. I f***ing knew it was you.'

I tried to keep things light and smiled. 'Sorry, mate?'

'I've been waiting to see you,' he continued.

'OK, is everything all right?'

'You f***ing steal from charity. You've stolen millions, you. You keep telling everyone you're giving it to food banks, but I've seen your accounts. I've seen what you earn and I know what you are.'

I just wanted to defuse it. I'm always very conscious not to aggravate.

'I don't want to get into a row, I'm just here for the football,' I said. 'But what you've said isn't true, mate.'

I left the queue, went back to my mates and said we needed to leave because there was a guy shouting the odds. He followed me.

'I've got all my mates here and we'll be waiting outside for you!' he said. And he walked out the door.

I had to ask the barman if he could help me get out safely because there was someone outside threatening to beat me up. He called the bouncers over to escort me to a taxi and there was a group of five or six lads all heckling and shouting.

'We'll f***ing get you next time we see you!' they yelled as I was bundled into a cab.

Rox

Mark didn't feel he could go back to Forest after that, despite the decades of loyal support. In my opinion, the club didn't do enough to support Mark attending games. I obviously don't understand how football grounds work, nor the complexities of the security, but there were very few avenues of support offered to Mark.

The only way he could feel safe in the ground after that was to pay to watch from the hospitality section, but then he got accused of thinking he was 'too good' to sit in the stands. For crying out loud, he was going to get the s**t kicked out of him if he'd stayed where he was. There was even someone within the hospitality area who would regularly share updates on

Twitter about their disgust at him being in there with them. It was gutting because football has always been Mark's way of switching off from life and all the digital noise and now even doing that was no longer possible.

Mark

My mental state was incredibly fragile. Hanging by a thread for much of the time. Every single interview I gave for that fifth Christmas started with the question of how much money went to the charity. I was terrified of saying something that could then be twisted to give the trolls more ammunition, just as had happened with the dredging up of the *Guardian* article.

Rox

We were getting threatening emails and DMs saying they had our address and were going to come round to the house because they knew what we were up to.

I couldn't go on like this and I insisted that we called the police.

Mark

A couple of days later, two plain-clothes officers visited the house and we told them everything that had been going on.

Unlike anyone from the police we'd spoken to before, they totally appreciated the situation and didn't make us feel like we were fussing over nothing.

Rox

They'd been online and seen for themselves how much s**t we were getting, and took it seriously. They arranged to come back a few days later and this time brought someone from the anti-terrorism unit. It had been escalated because of the level of trolling we were being subjected to, how influential our platform was and how many followers we had in the UK and around the world.

Mark
They sat with us and showed us how best to secure our channels to protect ourselves from as much of the hate speech as we could. We talked about ways to protect ourselves when we were out of the house as well.

Rox
They were such a reassuring presence. Someone was helping us a bit here and that felt good.

Mark
But also terrifying. Just by going for a Christmas number one, we ended up with anti-terrorism police at the house. Madness.

Rox
We logged everything with them and knowing they were aware of it and that we had some strategies in place to temper the situation made me feel a tiny bit safer.

Mark
That hadn't been the first time we'd called the police out that year. Bubbling away in the background to all this had been the blackmail attempts made on us over a hazy video that allegedly showed me in a bar with a girl.

Rox
Again, this is not something we've ever spoken about before, but we want to take it up now because we think it adds important context to the overall situation.

Mark

The messages had started in early 2022 via DM with an anonymous account saying they wanted five grand or else they were going to leak this video. We were used to the crank messages, especially since the Ed and Elton number one, and so we just ignored it.

Then the DMs moved to emails demanding ten grand and those messages now included the video clip, which we were seeing for the first time.

Rox

I knew it wasn't Mark in the film. He knew it wasn't him. The first thing he said was, 'That's not f***ing me', and he was incredibly disturbed by it. Trust is something we really pride ourselves on in our relationship and Mark doesn't lie. It was all so weird.

Mark

As far as we could make out, it was a fake video, possibly made with AI.

Rox

At no point would or could Mark have been in that situation. We don't go out without each other or alone these days so it wasn't a circumstance that could have happened. I knew this wasn't real – there were too many things that didn't add up.

We reported it to the police, but all the accounts vanished and there was no proof.

Mark

It was eventually posted to TikTok in the August and then some of the papers picked it up, which started some very upsetting speculation about our relationship.

Rox

And it was really hard to see Mark go through that because we're solid in our marriage. I'd get a lot of abuse too from people saying, 'No wonder he's doing that, you're too fat.'

Mark

We considered putting out a response, but we didn't want to highlight it further. As soon as you speak publicly about something, you more or less give the green light to the rest of the media and everyone else to run ahead with the story. It just snowballs.

We stuck to the strategy of fighting the negative with positive. Keep putting out good, don't give any oxygen to the trolls who had it in for us, and if people didn't like us or want to follow us, then that was up to them.

Rox

We were also aware that we were regularly being torn apart on a really dark internet forum that exists solely to destroy people in the public eye, often with the most outrageous slurs.

The pain that this website has caused for so many people is unreal.

Mark

The first time I'd come across it was during the trolling the previous year. Just a pit of s**t, post after post of sheer hatred. It made me question everything we were doing – was it seriously worth it to be subjected to this? And the hardest thing to read were the posts from people who we knew must be close to us in real life.

Rox

There was information in some of them that could only have come from friends or family and that was like a dagger to the heart.

Mark

When there are only a few people who know something specific and then it appears in a post on a forum like that ... it was such a betrayal. We never confronted anyone. It was easier just to step back and stop sharing anything with anyone. We became very closed off.

Even now, whether it's to do with family, health or work, we tend not to tell anyone anything.

Rox

It was a harsh lesson that not everyone wants you to succeed. Not everyone comes with you. And I feel like it's not their fault – that's the way I cope with it, anyway. They've perhaps not healed from something and that's their issue to deal with. But I can't take their feelings on any more.

Mark

It's savage when the insults aren't just about your professional business, but also your personality, looks and character. When I was a graphic designer, if somebody came over and said, 'I hate that website you've just built', I'd be upset, but I wouldn't go home and worry that I was a terrible person. Whereas if somebody says: 'I f***ing hate LadBaby because he's a dickhead', then that's a personal attack and it cuts much deeper.

Rox

They even talked about the children and the way they looked. It was such a stark thing to realise there were people out there who *really* hated us.

In the week the 'Food Aid' single was released, the Trussell Trust put out a statement in support of us, clarifying exactly how much we'd fundraised and brought to the charity.

'They've raised £1,305,000 for us through brand partner-ships and songs in total,' they wrote. 'With their number ones solely, they've raised a total of £305k for us. We're so grateful to LadBaby for helping us raise vital funds, but also awareness of the issues people locked in poverty are facing.'

Mark

The £305k part of the figure came from the record sales and the one million was from the donations we'd brought in via partnerships with Walkers and Pepsi.

But the Trussell Trust were also fighting fires about us on social media. No charity trying to help people feed their fam-ilies should be battling trolls online. As if they have time to do that. But they did it to defend us and they were also replying individually to people who were challenging them.

Rox

Someone was repeatedly asking them exactly how much money LadBaby had donated and they replied directly with the words from the statement.

Mark

It was decisive and I think that stopped a lot of the trolls in their tracks because these were facts from the charity itself. But although it gave some people pause for thought, it wasn't like the harassment ground to a halt.

Rox

I'm so sad that the story behind all the Christmas fundraising and charity work sounds so negative, because this was never how it was supposed to go. And there is a lot of it that we feel massively positive about. My heart could burst with pride over what we helped turn into a reality. But this is also part of the story. It happened to us. It was real.

Mark

I could never see those five songs as something awful because they remain the best thing we've ever done. I couldn't be prouder. But it came at a personal cost and it was the reason we stopped.

Rox

I knew I couldn't take this level of pain, stress and upset again. Emotionally and mentally, I didn't have it in me. Neither did Mark. I'd seen the impact on his mental health and the panic attacks, and how horrendous that was for our family. I was still terrified he was going to end up having a heart attack or a stroke.

Mark

It was the point of no return. There would be no more singles and this time we meant it.

16

Healing and Feeling

Rox
Without a single to promote, Christmas 2023 was wonderfully boring and we wanted to give our boys the family time they needed after the five years of chaos.

Mark
We did all our usual traditions, taking the boys to Winter Wonderland in London and visiting the Christmas lights on Oxford Street without having to try and squeeze all of that into a crazy promotional schedule.

Rox
We even managed to get all the presents wrapped a month early instead of the mad dash on Christmas Eve it had been for the last five years! We were able to see much more of friends and family. It was peaceful and calm and somewhat healing for us both.

Mark
Anyone who follows the charts might remember that Sam Ryder was going for the Christmas number one this time with his song 'You're Christmas to Me'. We met him in the middle of his campaign and he looked properly shattered.

Rox

Bless his heart. He had that unmistakable thousand-yard stare – the 'Christmas number one fatigue face' we knew only too well. You could see the absolute exhaustion in the poor man. Very few people know what those two weeks before Christmas are like when you're in a chart race. You hardly sleep, maybe a few hours a night at best.

Mark

We went on an Instagram Live with him on the Thursday night before the Official Chart came out, wishing him the best of luck and encouraging everyone to get behind him. He was cream-crackered. And he said he didn't know how we had physically done this five years running.

Rox

Despite his mammoth effort, Sam didn't quite make it to number one. In the end, Wham! finally got it, thirty-nine years after 'Last Christmas' was first released, with Sam's track coming in second.

And guess what? Even though I wouldn't have swapped places with him and I was glad that we had a relaxing Christmas without the commitments of a chart campaign, my heart still ached over the way it had ended. Creating those songs and knowing what a difference they were making was the most joyous thing in the world and not being able to do it any more was the saddest.

I'd loved seeing families singing along and people donating and getting involved. The Christmas spirit all of that generated had been incredible.

Mark

I'll be honest: when we put out the announcement in November 2023, confirming that after five amazing years, we were passing on the baton, it broke my heart. There was a new food bank opening in Nottingham that we went to visit and I felt guilty that we weren't doing a song that year. I couldn't shake it.

Emma Revie, the CEO of the Trust, told us that the largest amount of exposure for the charity over the last five years had come from our songs. We both felt such a huge sense of responsibility to keep them in the spotlight. Was it selfish of us to put ourselves first?

Rox

Mark found the November and December period very hard, like he should be doing something but wasn't able to. We were still supporting the Trussell Trust behind the scenes (we always will) but it left a big hole in our lives and we were acutely aware that this year they would be deprived of the lump sum raised from the songs.

All because of one sodding falsehood that had spiralled.

Mark

We worked hard to fill that financial gap. When we partnered with Pukka Pies to create a special-edition Christmas Dinner pie that winter, we made sure one of the conditions of the deal was that a portion of the sales went to the Trussell Trust.

Rox

We brought out another *Greg the Sausage Roll* book, which also raised funds for the charity. It was all about finding a way to replace the money from the Christmas songs.

Mark

We also did an awful lot of soul-searching and had learned a hell of a lot from the whole experience. Even though we'd been entrenched in the world of social media for a number of years by now and thought we had a handle on how it operated, it had been a real eye-opener into the realities of the industry. No one from the online world ever reached out to see if we were OK. Everyone stayed away.

Some of our friends were supportive but as far as the industry itself went, there was nothing. And I think it taught us that this is a lonely business.

Rox

When the going gets tough, social media is not very, well, 'social'. It might be different for creators who have teams around them, but that isn't something we have. It's always been just the two of us and the overall effect was to tighten our bond. Together, we're a powerhouse. This job can be lonely, but me and Mark have each other and I'm grateful for that.

As long as we're putting out positivity, creating imaginatively and doing what we think is right, then I have faith that things will turn out OK in the end.

Mark

It also taught me that I've got more resilience than I thought and it's made me even stronger.

I'm glad that we didn't give in when we could have done after the fourth single. I'm proud that we carried on through the fire because we knew we were doing the right thing and we believed in the project.

Rox

You know the Upside Down on *Stranger Things*? The alternative dimension that exists in parallel to the real world? That's how I see the internet sometimes.

Mark

I've tried to care less about what people think but I can't help it. I do care. I might be able to hide it better than I used to, but it always hurts. One of the basic premises for being successful online is being liked. So it's a weird place to be a lot of the time.

Rox

But are other people's opinions worth getting our knickers in a knot over? I don't want to change who I am. Not everyone has to like us and that's OK, I'm totally cool with that.

There's nothing any of us can do about someone else loving or hating us, so we might as well just ignore the carnage because otherwise it's taking on everyone else's emotions.

Mark

We recently had a review for our podcast that really made me laugh.

'Mark,' wrote this listener, 'I always thought you were a bit of a knob, but I loved Rox. I listened to season one and am obviously now on season two. You guys are great and really cheer up a grumpy HGV night driver. Honestly love it. Mark, I don't think you're a knob any more. Class, keep it up.'

Rox

We should get that printed on a canvas: 'Mark, I don't think you're a knob any more.'

Mark

Thing is, I don't really mind people thinking I'm a knob. I mean, I'd prefer it if they didn't! But as long as they don't think I'm a knob because I stole charity money, then I can live with it.

Rox

I think as we've gained experience, however difficult that has been, we're now able to weather the storms more quickly and move on.

Mark

We're desensitised to the worst of it, aren't we?

Rox

I reckon so. We have a cry, have a cuddle and then we crack on with life.

Mark

Another thing we've learned is that you can't win. For years I've had abuse over my teeth, but now that I've got an Invisalign retainer to straighten them out, some people think it's a sign of me 'changing' and losing touch with my working-class roots.

Rox

People make comments about my weight all the time. I tend to gain weight in the winter and lose it in the summer, it's just how I am with the seasons. But I'll get people telling me I'm too fat or too thin and that I'm disgusting. Or they'll talk about how 'annoying' I am or how much they hate my laugh.

Bullies and trolls will always exist, online and off it. And we don't need to put up with it, so we won't tolerate abuse towards us or our followers. This is a space that me and Mark have created and just as you wouldn't allow someone to come into your office and smash it up, we will protect our working space.

Mark

We don't have many people that we can talk to about our job, so me and Rox are probably closer than most couples. I know she gets it and vice versa.

Rox

We talk every night and that almost feels like our little form of therapy.

Mark

If I go to one of my best mates to offload about something that happened at work that day, it kind of falls on deaf ears. To them, I don't really 'work' and I completely understand why they think that. We don't do a nine to five, we don't clock in and clock out, we don't have a boss. I'm not doing twelve-hour shifts stacking shelves.

People who have known us for years still say: 'What do you actually *do*? I know you do the videos, but what's your job?'

And even now I find that question an awkward one to answer. Literally this morning, in Costa Coffee, just before we sat down to tackle this latest chapter, a couple of people came up to us and asked for selfies. There was a woman, probably in her sixties, who saw this happen and asked them who we were.

'Is he a footballer?' is what she said. True story.

Rox

That's a great compliment, love. I'd take that.

Mark

She'd clearly noticed what terrific shape I'm in!

Anyway, the people we'd taken a picture with told her we did social media videos and she came over and this time asked us directly who we were. This is what I always find difficult to pin down. I said we made funny videos online, raised money for charity and wrote children's books. It was only the books bit that she understood.

That happens a lot – when we mention *Greg the Sausage Roll*, people stop looking so bemused and say, 'Oh, you're an author!'

Rox

That's an easy one to grasp. It's like an accountant or a brick-layer. Our job never really sounds like anything official. Social media is not seen as an established industry, even though everyone uses it all day, every day.

Of course there are *waaaay* more challenging industries to work in. I'm not going to claim that what we do is tough manual labour. But we do put the hours in. We run all of the platforms ourselves – Facebook, Instagram, YouTube and TikTok – with Mark editing everything we upload and writing all the captions. The whole shebang.

We could never hand any of that over to someone else because no one edits like Mark or knows the LadBaby style better than him.

Mark
We're also control freaks!

Rox
But in a positive way.

Mark
We're not delegators, we prefer to do everything ourselves and then it's on us.

Rox
Oh my god, Mark, please never die! I can do Instagram edits – reels and story short form content – but my brain can't do any of the rest.

Mark
Thankfully, we'd had a multitude of Good Things to focus on throughout 2023 as we'd picked up the pieces and recovered. We celebrated hitting thirteen million followers across our channels. We launched our podcast, *Live, Laugh, Love*, which was shortlisted for the Listeners' Choice award at the British Podcast Awards, where we were also asked

to cover the backstage hosting duties. We released two more *Greg* books, published a further one for World Book Day 2024 and completed book tours across the country. We were invited to attend the Pride of Britain Awards and did live dates in Nottingham and Birmingham for *Live, Laugh, Love.*

Rox

And we continued putting out our content. Having been quite creatively stifled during the backlash, when we were both so consumed with what was happening to us, I found my passion again and rediscovered my love for making videos.

Mark

That shared passion for creating burns bright as ever. I feel safe on our channels. I know our audience and that you guys will be with us no matter what. I never have to second-guess you.

Rox

None of this has changed what I want to do in the world with Mark. We will continue to strive to put out positive content and to push the brands we work alongside to give back.

Social media is a hard place to be, but if you stick to who you are and what makes you happy, then it can be one of the most rewarding.

If someone wants to attack me for my weight, I'll take that negative energy and create something to inspire people. That might be a reel featuring some plus-size dresses for under twenty quid and if that helps other women who are my shape, my size and who are tired from mumming, and it stops them feeling how that troll wants me to feel, then I've turned that nastiness into a force for good.

In with anger and out with love. That's what works for me.

*

Can I just say how much I love our followers? I bloody *adore* every last one of you. The relationship we have is incredibly special and unique and it's still going strong, baby!

Mark

We've both found solace in the community we've built and who have been there for us through all the ups and downs.

Rox

I especially love how collaborative LadBaby has become. We get sent the most amazing ideas for couples' challenges or TikTok trends to try out. I get so many DMs about pranks to play on Mark and the scheming is epic.

Mark

Almost all the ideas for our stitch videos, where we attempt to recreate the most ludicrous acrobatic manoeuvres, have originated from followers begging us to please, please, please try and do this.

Rox

How we've not ended up in hospital properly hurt yet, I'll never know. You know we're eventually going to come a cropper on one of those, Mark.

Mark

We've not had any serious injuries, but we have started going to a chiropractor.

Rox

We'll go for the appointment and she's like, 'You been throwing him over your shoulders again?'

Mark

Or before we've even sat down she'll say: 'I saw the video. I know exactly why you're here and where you've got pain.'

Rox

We've invested in some crash mats now at least. We're not getting any younger.

Mark

Of all our platforms, Facebook feels most like home. That's where it all began. It's the Facebook audience who got us to where we are today.

Rox

And they are the audience who still turn up for us.

Mark

They've always shown up for us. Whatever we do, they get behind it. Similarly with Instagram, which I know Rox has a real affinity with.

Rox

I love the mums on there and the nature of Instagram feels very female, creative and visual. But we don't earn from Instagram, apart from through external brand deals.

Mark

We like YouTube, but it's not really a bill payer, either. We're not ridiculously popular on there, we never go massively viral. But neither does anything ever bomb. We're consistently middle of the road.

Rox

We're on TikTok, although it's fair to say neither of us are big fans.

Mark

I hate TikTok. There, I said it. You don't get to build a relationship with anyone. The people who 'know' us from there won't know our names. They won't even know we're LadBaby. We're 'the dancing couple from TikTok'.

Whereas people who know us from Instagram, Facebook and YouTube will see us in the street and go: 'Hi Mark, hi Roxy! Love your book, love your videos! How are you?'

Rox

It's just a different level of engagement.

Mark

We were very late joining TikTok. But staying away was becoming bad from a business point of view because it's often part of brand contracts to post content across Facebook, Instagram and TikTok. Brands are particularly focused on TikTok and if we're not on there, they want to know why.

So we're there because we have to be as part of the job, but it doesn't feel like a natural fit for us.

Rox

Kids would be more competent, in my opinion . . .

Mark

Keeping on top of the different platforms and making sure our content gets seen is an ever-evolving task.

Rox

But you could drive yourself mad trying to keep pace with the algorithms. I've known creators who have run themselves into the ground chasing all the 'rules', which can change at the click of a button, and still not managed to get the engagement or exposure they need to survive. So we try not to get bogged down in all that and instead remain consistent and true to ourselves.

Mark

We're always there or thereabouts. A constant for people. I like that.

Rox

Authenticity is what people value the most. The people who follow us have seen us grow and know the truth. Stay who you are because that's what makes you unique.

Mark

If we're not physically working on something, we're thinking about it, which isn't unusual when you have your own business. I don't feel that we're ever turned off from it. Do you, Rox?

Rox

Nah. We're always on. Even going on holiday, I find it difficult to put my phone in the safe and be separated from it. I've tried doing that in the past and I got bored! I like to create things and to keep busy and involved and pressing pause on that isn't something I do very well.

Mark

We're often asked how we manage the boys' internet access and decide how much of them to share, and it really is an ongoing process. I would never claim to have that figured out – like every parent out there at the moment, we're learning as we go. But as far as appearing on camera goes, it's completely led by them.

Rox

They're still young and we know that as they get older they might find what we do embarrassing. You never know, it could happen! So we say they can be in the video if they want but there's never any pressure.

Mark

They're such different characters though, aren't they?

Rox

We always say that Phoenix looks like Mark but is me in personality whereas Kobe looks like me but is Mark in personality. Nix is very sociable and outgoing and a bit more of a diva. He loves the limelight and having his photo taken and wants to be in every video.

Mark

Kobe is much more quiet and shy and has no interest in having his picture taken. He'd much rather be outside digging a hole or kicking a ball or climbing a tree. Phoenix is much more safety conscious and will want to hand sanitise if his hands are sticky. Kobe would eat mud and lick the floor if we let him!

Rox

The boys might be opposites but they are so close and they bring out the best in each other. But that's why you won't see Kobe in our videos as much. He just doesn't care about all that and it's not something we want to make him do.

Obviously we also want to protect them as much as we can from the harmful side of being online. They don't have phones or social media. I would never want them to experience an ounce of the negativity we have. I never want them to be trolled; the thought of that happening makes my heart hurt.

Mark

Our boys know how to use YouTube, they know how to type in and find the videos they like. Kobe loves *Fireman Sam* and he knows how to find him.

I'm completely happy with them being on YouTube. It might not be our biggest platform personally, but it's the one I have the most respect for because of their guidelines. They have everything rigidly in place, they take down harmful content swiftly, put age restrictions on certain videos and they really helped us when we were trolled. They were the best. We still have the same partner manager at YouTube we've had from the beginning.

But love it or hate it, social media is going to be a huge part of their lives as it is for everyone.

Rox

Everything is done on your phone now. Banking, shopping, booking travel, GP appointments. You can't even park your car without paying for it via an app.

Mark

You can even open locked doors – soon we'll not even need keys. The technology is only going to get more sophisticated and we want the boys to be ready for all of that.

Rox

We'll just have to constantly monitor it as they get older; that's what we're trying to do. As much as I would love to, we can't wrap them in cotton wool for ever, but we can give them the tools to protect themselves.

Our job as parents is to educate them and make them aware of how to use the platforms safely, and to give them the confidence and resilience to manage that.

That doesn't mean caving in and giving them a phone as soon as they ask for one, though.

I was the last one in my year to get a phone and I hated that, but I understand why my parents did that now. I remember being aged fifteen and so desperate for a Nokia because I wanted to play Worm.

Mark
Snake, Rox. Snake.

Rox
Oh yeah, Snake! You knew what I meant.

Mark
For all the bumps in the road, there's no doubt that doing this job has taken us to the most weird and wonderful places. We don't see ourselves as 'celebs' and so to find ourselves invited to lavish red-carpet events like the 2024 BAFTAs is mind-boggling.

Rox
Me and Mark, swanning down the red carpet, rubbing shoulders with Jeff Goldblum. Who even are we?! Was this actually happening?

Mark
Rox turns into her nan at awards ceremonies. For everyone who wins, she's like, 'Aw, I bet their parents are so proud!'

Rox
I can't help it. I just think of their mum and nan at home watching on the telly.

I do love an awards do, although the pressure was on for the BAFTAs because that red carpet is the British fashion moment of the year and all eyes are on you for the few minutes you're posing for the paps. I always keep my clothes affordable – I'm much more comfortable in high street anyway – and found a beautiful gold dress from Goddiva for £78 that made me feel like a million dollars.

Mark

Rox knows how to work a red carpet. She knows how to pose, she knows her best side, her hair's always great, makeup's perfect, she looks directly down the lens. Stunning.

Me, on the other hand . . . Because of my height, I look awkward next to other human beings at the best of times. Put me in a suit and a pair of funeral shoes and it's even worse because I don't even know how to stand. Shall I go for hands in pockets or a slouchy lean? What should my face be doing? Mean and moody or cheesy grin?

Rox

Mark always ends up looking like he's searching in the distance for his lost dog.

Mark

We'll get comments on the photos saying, 'Yep, Mark's lost his dog again!'

Rox

I thrive off the red-carpet adrenaline from all the energy and happy vibes. Posing for the paps as they shout your name ('Rox! Over here!') is an assault on all the senses, but for one night every once in a while, I get to feel like a Hollywood star.

Mark

I enjoy bits of all that, but it's not my natural habitat. I was much more at home afterwards when we came out of the Royal Festival Hall and headed to McDonald's on the Embankment. Rox in her gold dress and me in my suit.

Rox

We had a lovely burger and some chicken nuggets and it was the perfect way to end the night. Me and Mark always end up with a fast food burger after these posh dos. It's Mark's highlight.

Mark

And then the next day I'll be back in my trackies putting the bins out. It's a funny old world.

Rox

We're both very lucky, but equally grateful.

Mark

LadBaby has taken us both to places we never expected. When we started all this, I wouldn't even have got up at the local karaoke and I'd barely read a book. So to have sung on five number-one singles and become a bestselling children's author is hysterical.

And it's the things that have taken us out of our comfort zone that have turned out to be the best experiences, so whenever an opportunity comes in, I want to go for it, challenge myself and keep this crazy train going.

Rox

It's true that the most uncomfortable projects have been our biggest successes.

Mark

Right! I want to be pushed into more uncomfortable places.

Rox

Well, I can certainly help you with that!

Mark

Classic Rox.

17

The Future

Mark

Where does LadBaby go from here? All I know is that I don't want to slow down. I enjoy that our life is a bit chaotic and we never quite know what's coming around the corner.

Rox

I'd love to turn our story into a movie!

Mark

We get asked a lot about whether we'd ever go on a reality show and it would be great to tick that box. We've had talks with *I'm a Celebrity* and *Dancing on Ice* in the past, but no formal approaches. They have our contact details and we're always open to any conversation.

Rox

If *Strictly* came knocking, I'd jump at the chance! But there's still not a lot of crossover between social media and main-stream media and I don't think we're the sort of people that telly naturally embraces.

Also, I think we're so lucky to have the space we do and I don't particularly want to jeopardise that for a place in the jungle or a shot at the Glitterball Trophy. We've bounced back from what happened and it makes you think about your life in a different way. We survived that and now we want to be there for our kids, to appreciate the present, to *be* present and really enjoy what we're doing.

Mark

Rox did some presenting on *Lorraine* and we have a really good, ongoing relationship with the show, so hopefully she can do some more of that in the future.

Rox

That was a really positive experience. I was like a roving Bridget Jones, where they'd phone up and say, 'Hey, do you want to get in a giant zorb and be kicked around an England pitch with the Lionesses?'

Sure, I'm your girl!

'Fancy fighting a troll at Warwick Castle, Rox?'

Sign me up!

I want to keep trying new things and innovate and I pray that we can carry on doing what we do and making these wonderful memories.

Mark

We're passionate about passing on our knowledge of the industry to others who need a bit of guidance, as well. Last year, YouTube asked us to go into their offices because they were having a big meeting with organisations including the NHS, the fire service, the police and the army about how they could use social media to better connect with the public. We were brought in to be part of those conversations.

Rox

I love that side of where we're at now, being able to help train the people coming up behind us. I get a lot of celebrities and personalities online asking for advice on improving their social media engagement and I'm always happy to provide that if I can.

Mark

A lot of people contact us when they've just gone viral or if someone has offered them a deal.

If nothing else, I hope we're proof of what can happen if you go for your dreams. The biggest and the best dreams often take a lot of hard work and energy, but they are also the ones most worth fighting for.

Rox

Dreams don't become reality overnight. But without the journey, there's no story to tell. Never giving up, staying true to who you are and believing in yourself are what build character and integrity.

Mark

Nothing would ever get done if everyone was scared of failing. Sometimes our videos flop and that's OK. It doesn't matter and I know that now. What actually matters is being able to move on, not allowing that to dictate the rest of your day or week and bearing in mind that even the setbacks are part of the process.

We have been offered opportunities off the back of videos that underperformed or are several years old and long forgotten. You never know what anything will eventually lead to.

Rox

People often equate success to money and status, but it really can come in many different forms. It might be finding a career that gives you more time with your family. I'm not interested in driving a Ferrari or prancing about with a Birkin bag. Fair play if that's what you want to do, but I measure success by what actually makes me happy rather than what other people tell me to be happy about it.

Mark
Wise words, Rox. Most of all, we both want to keep having fun, don't we?

Rox
Abso-bloody-lutely. I'm looking forward to whatever the future holds and we hope you guys will stick around to see what's coming, too.

If the last few years are anything to go by, there's not going to be a dull moment.

Mark
We wouldn't have it any other way.

The Last Word

To say we've both been nervous about writing this book and sharing our story would be the understatement of the millennium.

We're always determined to spread positivity and happiness and we know that's why people have stuck by us all these years. And at the heart of this book – we hope! – is an uplifting, feelgood story that is worth celebrating.

But, as you'll now know, there has been another side to it. Social media only ever gives you a snapshot of people's lives and we wanted to write this book to show you who we are, where we've come from, what makes us tick. And so that has meant delving into some painful parts of our past, opening up wounds that are barely healed and revealing more about ourselves than we ever thought we would.

Yikes. It's not always been easy, we promise you that!

But getting everything out in the open and having the opportunity to speak our truth has been like therapy because we've been holding on to a lot of this stuff for too long. Yes, we're apprehensive about the fact that people are going to know our innermost thoughts and feelings, but it's also been a hell of a relief to put it all out there.

Like this huge weight has lifted.

You might remember the video we made earlier this year to announce the book was coming out. We went back to a park near where we used to live in Hemel Hempstead to record it because it was a place we both remembered as somewhere we used to visit at a time when we were struggling financially.

It's a beautiful, peaceful space with a cricket pitch, daffodils in the spring and a little lake. When we were there, we could forget about our worries for a while.

Going back was so weird because the last time we'd been there, life had looked very different. Our money problems were so dire, there had been a very real possibility of us losing the house. We remember one Saturday in 2017, the two of us were sitting in this park eating buttered pasta out of a Tupperware while Phoenix happily played in the sunshine. The juxtaposition of his innocent joy with our fears about the future is something that has stuck with both of us, so it felt fitting, in a 'full circle' sense, to return there for the book announcement.

You'll have seen that we were emotional wrecks! But the response from you guys was simply incredible. We were inundated with positive messages of support and after the hurt of the last couple of years, that reaction restored our faith in humanity.

So, from the bottom of our hearts, thank you (again!) for that. Whatever happens, we are proud beyond words of this book.

We've also enjoyed going all the way back to our childhoods, school days and university years and reliving our misspent youths! And remembering getting together and falling in love has been a beautiful thing.

We'd really like Phoenix and Kobe to read it one day when they're old enough to understand. We love that the boys will always have this account of our early lives, how we met and where this has taken us as a family.

Because while the LadBaby journey has been challenging at times, it's also been phenomenally joyous and we feel so fortunate to be here. There's a lot of worry and pain in the world, we know that. But there is also hope, and people tell us all the time that our videos give them a lift when they most need one.

Just today we met a woman who had been listening to the podcast. Her husband died a couple of years ago and she was finding the pod a great source of comfort because the two of us reminded her of the relationship she'd had with her late husband. That had made her smile and she said it felt like we were with her.

That's golden to us.

And it's what we hope this book will do for people – we've always said that we want everyone to come on the ride with us. The last eight years have been crazy, exhausting, hilarious, exciting and emotional beyond belief. And we couldn't have done any of it without you.

Thank you for being our family. Sorry if that sounds cheesy, but we don't say it lightly. We reckon we share a bond with our audience that is built on respect, understanding and a shared love of laughter. It just works, doesn't it?

Without even realising it, you have helped us through everything. From the insecurities about being new parents, to worrying about whether we're bringing the kids up well, to supporting us in the charity campaigns and then in our darkest moments with the trolling. Most of you we've never even met, but every one of you has held us up and pushed us forward, at times even more so than our own friends and family.

When things have felt bleak, knowing we've had this amazing gang of awesomeness behind us has kept us going.

We're not exceptional people. We've just achieved some extraordinary things through dedication, hard work and a little bit of luck. And we are never not grateful for the opportunities and experiences you guys have made possible for us.

We still love what we do every single day. We still get the

same buzz out of making a funny video as we did way back at the beginning.

We know other social media creators who long for the day when they don't have to do it any more. They can't bear the thought of doing this for ever. They find the pressures too great, the competition too fierce and the negativity too overwhelming.

They want to put their feet up and not have to think about this digital world ever again.

We've never felt that. Not even close. We're only getting started! And this book feels like the perfect closure to an incredible chapter.

Now, let's see where the next one takes us . . .

With love,
Mark and *Rox*

Yesss, Maaaaaaaaaaaaaate! ;)

Acknowledgements

We would love to take this moment to express our deepest gratitude and thanks to Beth Neil, whose unwavering support and guidance made this book possible. As two dyslexic authors, the writing process has been locked in our heads for so long and presented us with so many challenges just to put pen to paper, but Beth's patience, encouragement and belief in our story helped us to overcome everything that stood in our way.

Her incredible feedback and collaboration were invaluable in being able to shape our story for the book and transform it into something we are so incredibly proud of. She never wavered in her dedication to making our voices heard, and we are immensely grateful for her commitment and at times being a shoulder to cry on. Thank you, Beth, for being a true champion of our dream and giving us the space and confidence to tell our story.

Lots of love,
Mark and *Rox*

PS: To Mark's university lecturer who never believed in him: I've still never watched *Breakfast at Tiffany's* and *Rocky* is still my favourite film!